THE FINANCIAL ADVISER

How to be a Successful Practitioner

Second Edition

Ian Green

ISBN: 978-1-7169-2904-5 (sc)
ISBN: 978-1-7169-2903-8 (e)

Lulu Publishing Services rev. date: 05/22/2020

"There's a saying 'When the student is ready, the book shows up.' What does this mean? Well, when we make changes, we chance upon pearls of wisdom, which seem as if they've been written just for us. and that is what this book is about. Ian Green, a forward thinking, enthusiastic practitioner, guides us through new ideas for sales and business management which really work and help improve our productivity"
Helen Jenkins, MLIA(dip), DipLS,
Chair, European Zone, Million Dollar Round Table

"Ian Green's book is a treasure chest of practical ideas to give your practice a boost. They're fun and easy to put to use. And, they're designed for sales people who know they need to be better business persons but who can't put up with overly complicated record keeping."
John Cruikshank
Past President, MDRT

"A great book from a great adviser. Ian has managed the very difficult task in writing a book about success in the financial services profession; making it effective and interesting to read. Ian bridged this easily with personal stories and hard examples of how to build a successful practice in a very short time. I have been fortunate to work closely with Ian on many occasions and his passion for this profession is evident in everything he does. He is willing to give of his time because his proven practices keep his business running efficiently while he is away. His adaptation and use of the points system and color coding systems are worth reading alone. Few in our profession have given more at such a young age and his passion will help you whether you are just starting or wanting to make that next leap in your practice."
Brian D. Heckert, CLU, ChFC
Past President, MDRT

INTRODUCTION

WHAT I DID IN ONE YEAR BUT NOT THE PREVIOUS FOUR

This book is not theory. It is not mumbo – jumbo. Everything in here really works. How can I be so sure? Because I did it! This book is really the story of one year of my life, using all the information I learned from books, tapes, seminars and colleagues in the Financial Services profession. Up until that fateful year I had been great at the theory of being a financial adviser and not bad, but not good, at putting it into practice.

I had often come away from a conference or read a book and been swamped with great but often too many ideas. I used to wonder where to start or would try to implement too many ideas at once with the inevitable result of soon falling back into my old ways. To combat this and to ensure that it doesn't happen with this book, I have distilled many of the ideas and concepts into one planner that fits onto one piece of paper. I call it 'The Success Plan' and over the coming chapters I'll provide all the ingredients for you to create your own Success Plan.

But to return to the story of how this book came about, as is so often the case in life, circumstances forced my hand.

In just one year I was married, witnessed the birth of my first son, moved to a new house and started my own company as an Independent Financial Adviser. The only one of life's traumatic events I didn't experience was death, and I intend putting that one off for as long as possible! Because of these events I suddenly had to work smarter. I only spent eight and a half months in the office that year, so unless I wanted to see a 33% reduction in my income, I had to do something.

What I did was put into practice everything I had learned in the previous four years. Of course, I was already doing some of it, some of the time but not in a structured fashion or with any consistency.

The great thing about the information in this book is that it doesn't matter what level you are at now, it will still work. You may be just starting out and need to know what to do to get going, or you may have many years experience but have reached a plateau in your production. Whatever your situation, this book will work for you.

Another reason I am so sure that it will work is because all the ideas and concepts have stood the test of time. Sure, a few of the ideas are mine but there are a lot that have been learned at UK Life Insurance Association (LIA) conferences, regional meetings and USA Million Dollar Round Table (MDRT) meetings. In addition, I have been an avid reader of books and by that I mean that I buy books and actually read them, rather than simply gaze at an attractive shelf of unopened volumes.

Finally, I have always made sure that I have been around great people. The phrase 'standing on the shoulders of giants' has never been truer. There are many great names in our industry who can tell of years of struggle or mediocrity before 'making it'. From the outset I wanted to avoid that, so I searched out and modelled myself on only the best. This paid off with 'overnight success' in just five years. By reading this book, and implementing all the ideas in it, you will be able to shorten that time further still.

It is popular these days for rock and pop groups to have 'tribute' or 'cover' bands. Two that spring to mind are Bjorn Again for ABBA and the El Beats who cover the Beatles. As well as that, many of the current chart hits by teen bands are simply cover versions of old records. In the cinema we are seeing films remade for the new millennium but with today's stars in the leading roles.

In many ways that is how I see this book. Although for lots of the sales ideas and business management concepts I am not the 'original artist', I hope you still enjoy the 'digitally enhanced' version I have recorded. Where I am aware of the 'original artist' I have indicated this and listed the source in Appendix A. Even though I have done my best to trace all sources the mists of time have shrouded some. If I have missed anyone out it is therefore through accident rather than malice and not for want of trying, so please accept my apologies if this is the case. To finish the media analogy, just like all the best album sleeves, I have included a 'thanks' Appendix at the back of this book listing some of the people and sources that have helped me on my way.

I hope you enjoy the book and that you succeed in every way you wish.

Ian Green
May 2002

HOW TO USE THIS BOOK

Contents:

A background to the book

A refresher course on the basics

How to kick-start your production

How to write a business plan

How to master your diary

How to control your finances

Who should read it: New advisers or those who feel their production levels have stagnated

Contents:

A step by step proven daily plan to instantly transform your business and working practices

How to guarantee a continuous stream of quality prospects via referrals and other methods

The daily points system

Who should read it: Advisers wanting to double production in less than a year or to work fewer hours

SECTION 1

CHAPTER 1

IN THE BEGINNING

As so often happens in life, what appears disastrous at the time can often be the catalyst for a wonderful change.

The start to my life insurance career was typical of many others. Up until that point I had been happy in my profession as a computer graphics designer, doing mostly conference presentations for large financial institutions such as merchant banks and the accounting and legal profession involved in the periphery of that industry.

I was a keen sportsman in my spare time and a horrific sports injury put paid to my design career. My arm was very badly broken and it became apparent that I would no longer be able to operate a computer and earn my living through that medium any more. For the first time in my life I was unemployed. There wasn't much I could do other than sit and read books or the daily newspaper. It was in one of the broadsheets one day in June that I spotted a small advert looking for individuals who wanted to work in the city with the potential for target earnings of £40k+. Wow! That was nearly three times what I had been earning in the computer graphics field and I had always fancied myself as a stockbroker. Due to the client roster at the graphics company I thought I knew more than most about futures, options, longs and shorts and P/E ratios.

It was only after I had been through the second interview (out of seven in total) that I realized this wasn't stocks and shares and being a city whiz kid but selling life insurance. However, by this point I had been sold the dream and was determined to make it. Despite being ridiculed for the clothes I turned up in, being laughed at about my haircut and suffering ritual humiliation at the hands of the branch manager in the final meeting, I was taken on! And so it was in September, five months after breaking my arm, that I became a trainee at a large Tied Agency.

For one week I stayed in the office, learning where things were kept and who my peer group would be. Then I was packed off to a hotel for two weeks of intensive (ahem!) training in the basic products of the life company and one week cramming for the FPC1 exam to be sat on the last day along with an observed role play just to be sure that I was safe to be released upon the great British public.

During those two weeks we were tested every morning on the previous days content and I made it my goal to be top of the class each day. This didn't mean that while the others were in the bar I was locked in my room all night but I made sure I didn't party until the work was done. Once back at our respective offices dotted around the country I kept in touch with a few of my class. It wasn't long before most had dropped out and I sometimes wonder what became of them. I hope they have found success in other fields, but the high turnover of staff can't have been good for my host company. This thought was confirmed when a few years later they sold what remained of the salesforce and closed their doors to new business.

In the last section of the book I'll document what happened to me along the way up until the moment of writing these words so that readers can hopefully use my experiences to their advantage.

I often think back to the individual who injured me so intentionally and badly, in a supposedly friendly game of sport, and quietly thank him! His act of brutality changed my life and opened up the world to me. I wonder where he is now ...?

CHAPTER 2

BACK TO BASICS

There is an old story about a life insurance branch manager who welcomes a new recruit into his office on his first day after completing basic sales training. The manager takes the arm of the new recruit and motions for him to follow. As they pass along the office the new recruit notices the sharp tailored suit and immaculately polished hand stitched shoes of the manager. They pass out of the building and get into the manager's car, a brand new, shiny, sports model. The manager presses a button and electronically lowers the roof and they speed out into the countryside, music playing on the expensive stereo system. They pull up to a large house and wrought iron gates swing silently open. The car crunches up a gravel path and pulls to a standstill outside a magnificent home. The manager gets out and leads the adviser to an ornate bench by the swimming pool. They sit down and the new recruit surveys the landscape, admiring the trappings of success around him. At this point the manager finally speaks. "Son, if you do what I say, if you put in the hours, if you make the sacrifices, if you make the calls, if you see the people and if you close the sales, one day all this ..." The manager takes a lingering look at the luxury items dotted around. "... all this, could be MINE"

An amusing story, but for those that have experienced the management system with its overrides and clawbacks, a story with more than a small element of truth in it.

My manager was a hard taskmaster. Hard, but fair. I had a great deal of respect for him and he had given me a chance. As long as I didn't annoy him, he didn't annoy me. If I asked for help, he gave it unconditionally, and for that I will be eternally grateful. When I came to leave his team to become an IFA, just five short months later he respected my decision and didn't really try too hard to stand in my way. For that I will always be grateful. He taught me the first concept that built my discipline. He called it the bible of time. This meant that if I wanted to speak with him, I had to book it in his diary and it had to be between 9am and 10am or 12 and 1pm or 4 and 5pm. At any other time I was supposed to be seeing prospects face to face or prospecting on the telephone. As you can imagine this was a harsh wake-up call. I had no prospects, except for a few friends and family and the only time I could contact my manager, the one man who could help me, was very rigid. It would also be the case that any time I saw him he would want to know how many people I had seen or called, so my figures had to be good or I was in trouble. Likewise, I'd be in trouble for asking stupid (in his eyes) questions, so I had to learn fast. While I am not advocating running a dictatorship, the discipline of a tightly run diary is one that I highly recommend and elaborate on later in this book. By being thrown in at the deep-end I had to learn to swim.

This bible of time concept has raised its head in many forms in various time management concepts over the years and is one I have used in a modified version to run my diary for the last three years. By always doing certain things at certain times they quickly become a habit and cease to be difficult. This was certainly the case with the method I was told I had to use to build my client base, that of cold calling. At first making forty cold calls a day made me feel ill! I would barely be able to go to sleep on a Sunday as the sick feeling in my stomach at the grind of the week ahead with its constant rejection kept me awake.

But I did not intend to fail and one of my colleagues took it upon himself to help me with the psychology of the telephone and where to obtain lists of people who would be interested in my new 'script'. To this day he is probably one of the main reasons I continued and decided that failure was not an option.

I quickly became an expert on the telephone. Cold calling is not something I'd necessarily advocate in today's world but nevertheless the skills I learnt have stood me in good stead today as the telephone remains one of the main tools of our trade. I number some of my best clients and friends among those I originally cold called in the early days.

The majority of my peers treated me, as a new trainee, with disgust and contempt. I understand now that all they were doing was continuing a chain of behaviour, echoing how they were treated themselves as trainees. As my production went past theirs and my trainee status was left behind, the snide comments soon faded. There were a few among the 60 or so people that worked in the large open plan office that I liked and remain friends with to this day.

It was by associating and learning from these select few advisers, who had a great work ethic and treated their clients well, that I learned the basics. By avoiding the 'coffee machine' or 'water cooler' crowd I avoided the negativity that proves the downfall of so many new entrants to this business.

It was at this time that I was introduced to the old-fashioned idea of the 'perfect sale', with an opening, a few stages in the middle and repeatedly 'closing' until the prospect gave up and said yes! Not too useful in the new millennium with an educated public wanting sound financial planning advice. But alongside this outdated concept I was also introduced to the concept of the sales circle (see Diagram 2.1) which still holds true today. No matter what new distribution channels open, no matter how much the internet and direct sales take off I believe that there will always be a requirement from a large number of people in the world for a face to face meeting with an adviser. And while that remains true, the sales circle will still need to be completed.

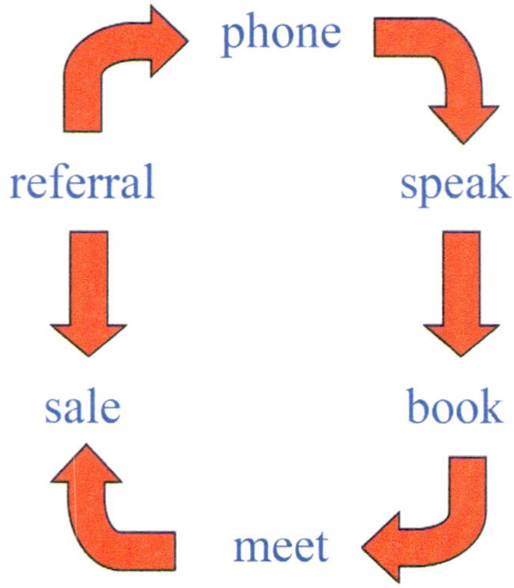

Diagram 2.1 – The Sales Circle

The sales circle starts with picking up the telephone, or increasingly in the modern world, access the email. The basic truth of the matter is that the more times we carry out this simple task, the more successful we are. I learnt of the sales circle five years ago, there were people teaching it fifty years ago and it will still be true in fifty years time.

Having made contact, we need to speak with the prospect and be able to interest them enough in our reason for calling in order to book a meeting. The meeting then needs to be held and we have to establish a level of trust before a sale can be made.

Finally, we need to obtain a referral so that the circle is complete and we have a new name to call on. So simple, yet so often forgotten, as we strive to avail ourselves of the latest technology, next great sales tip or up-to-date technical knowledge. All important factors, but of no use if we have no names to call and nothing to talk about.

CHAPTER 3

HOW TO GET GOING (AGAIN?)

I am a great believer in referrals, earned by client respect, and Chapter 6.5 is dedicated to just that. However, we all need to get started somewhere. As I wrote earlier the method forced on me was cold calling. There really is nothing wrong with this method but it takes a little time to master and understand that the inevitable rejection is not personal. Although a large number of calls can be made the success rate is not high and I would suggest best left to telesales professionals. As financial advisers our time may be better utilised gaining skills in other areas.

If you really are brand new and want to call people, but have absolutely no names at all, you may want to start with those around you, your friends, family and former colleagues. If you prefer a more remote approach consider purchasing a data list where names cost around 30p each (consisting of your pre-defined target market, more of which later) or joining an association and approaching its members, assuming this is allowed.

Any name that you have a connection with, no matter how tenuous is better than a straight cold call. If the name has previously bought from you or your company in some way then that is a great start. I know of lots of advisers who have a large client database of names yet still worry constantly about new business.

If you are new and already have some names, perhaps you have inherited a client base or been given a list of 'orphans'. If you are experienced and already have a client base but are unsure about calling or what to say to develop more business you will undoubtedly be familiar with that feeling (usually at the start of a month) of not knowing where the next piece of business is coming from. Here is how to banish that feeling forever:

The solution is an opportunity grid (note: Appendix A-1). Look at Diagram 3.1. To create your own, take a large sheet of squared paper or open a new file on your computer spreadsheet. Across the top write the names of all the products you sell. Down the side, write the names of all your prospects or clients.

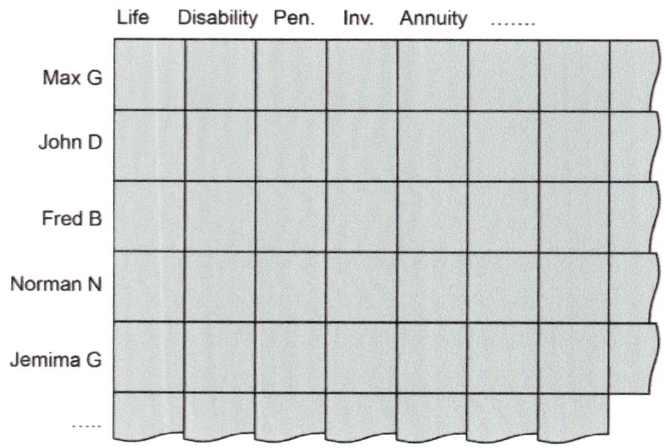

Diagram 3.1 – The Opportunity Grid

Then any product which a client has bought, colour in the square red. Any squares which may not be relevant, colour in black (for example a young single person may have no need for life cover and a retiree will have no need for retirement saving). Now work through all the gaps colouring any appropriate boxes in red or black. If a box is blank, there is no excuse for not phoning someone with a compelling reason to see us. You first of all enquire if they have the product, then if they need the product. If they have it, send a letter of authority to take over the agency and if not book a meeting to discuss it.

If you speak to someone and tell them about a product but they have not bought it yet, colour in half the box.

The real key to kick-starting your career or re-energising your business is if you have a lot of gaps, i.e. not coloured red or black, under one type of product. If that is the case, consider a mailshot or campaign. (see Diagram 3.2) For example if you find that not many people have a particular investment product then arrange for a company specialising in that product to provide you with a sample letter and generic product information so that you can complete a mailing. Follow up the mailing with a carefully thought out phone call and you will be amazed at the number of appointments that follow. This is because you have already identified a need of the prospect/client and you have a genuine, honest reason for meeting. As long as you then obtain basic details about the prospect, such as date of birth, you can also attend the meeting with a specific illustration prepared.

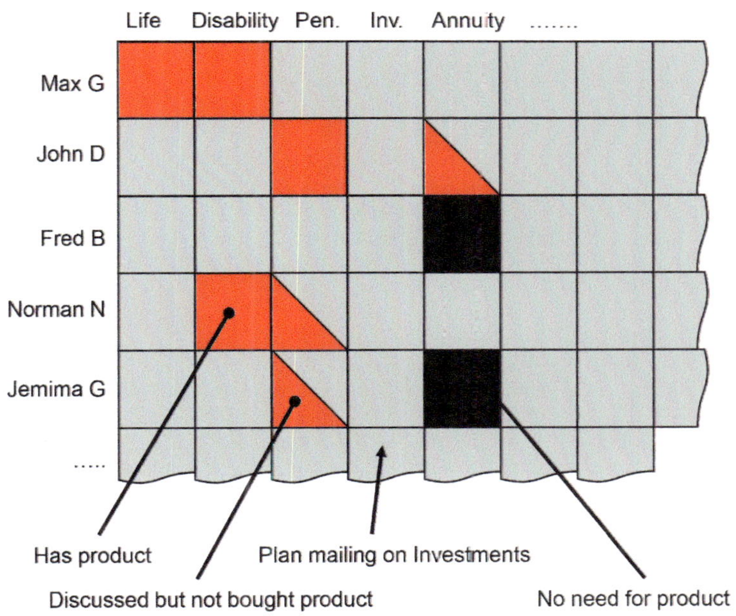

Diagram 3.2 – The Opportunity Grid

Put this grid up on the wall in your office where staff and clients can see it. Remember it has no figures on it so no breach of confidentiality occurs. If you are concerned, simply use client initials only. When clients come in they will often ask what the chart is. Explain, showing them their line and pointing out the lack of red boxes! Offer to give them a print out of their line or print their line and display it on the front of their file. You will find they start asking for new products so they can complete their line and even that clients who know each other compete to see who can have the most boxes!

This opportunity grid is an excellent tool to use at the start of a new year, to determine where our initial efforts should be concentrated and to banish those January 1 blues about where the work will come from.

It can also be used in many other ways, for example to determine training needs and schedules. Across the top, write down areas of expertise which you are yet to acquire. Down the left list all the staff names. Then colour in the boxes and maybe add dates as training is given. This grid can then form an integral part of your Training and Competency (T&C) file.

You may wish to use the grid to list mutual business opportunities across the top and professional introducers down the side, sending a regular mailing to the introducers on the various ways in which you could work together, or in other words using the grid to track your education of the introducers.

I am sure you can think of even more ways to use it and I'd be delighted to hear of any that work for you.

This concept, brought to 3D-life can also be used to break into new markets, such as the business owner. Often the trouble with making contact with a non-referred lead, especially those higher up the corporate ladder (and therefore harder to reach) is actually speaking with the right person. This so-called 'gatekeeper' was often the bane of my life in cold calling days. The following idea usually results in a conversation with the target prospect.

The Jigsaw

Buy a simple wooden childrens jigsaw, with approximately 6–10 pieces only.

Take the same piece out of all of them, put it to one side and send the rest of the jigsaw to your prospects. Remember, if you really don't have any prospects, you should decide on your target market, e.g. local owner/

entrepreneur businesses and obtain a list of them. You can buy these lists or make it yourself by walking around with a pen and paper and your eyes open! Simply decide who you would like as a prospect and approach them with the jigsaw mailing.

Then follow up with a call, explaining you are the person who sent the jigsaw. Most recipients will then be bursting to tell you there was a piece missing (proud that they attempted to complete it!). Go on to explain you have the missing piece and would like a few minutes of their time to explain why you sent it.

When you subsequently meet the prospect, produce a picture of a jigsaw showing the products you sell (see Diagram 3.3). Ask them to tick off any of the pieces they already have (life, disability etc).

Then explain you would like to work with them on the missing pieces.

Also explain that the jigsaw has no edges, and no picture on the box. This is because it is ever growing, and because it has no edges and no picture, they'll need the help of a jigsaw expert – you! By purchasing your services you will help them to get the full picture, provide more pieces as required and remove those that don't fit any more.

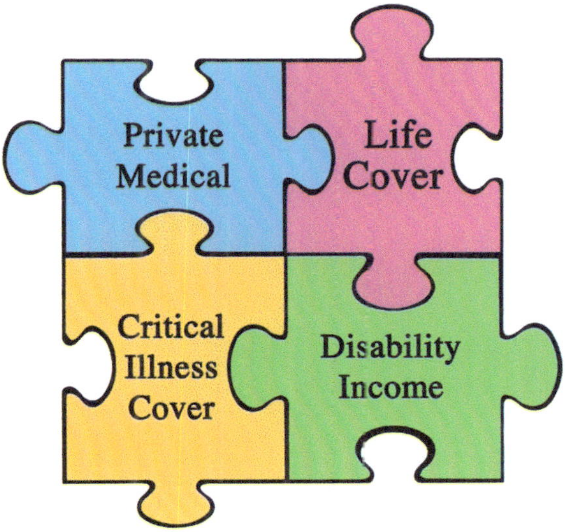

Diagram 3.3 – The Jigsaw

The example shows just four products. Yours can have as many pieces as products you are able to advise on.

There are pieces they don't need yet (long term care for young clients etc) and there are pieces they will need that haven't been invented yet (new products, changes in tax law) so always recommend that you and they stay in touch regularly.

Once you have completed business and they are a client, send a revised copy of the jigsaw, showing what they have and what is missing with brief details of what the missing pieces are and premiums for your recommendations.

You will find clients start calling to explain they want to purchase another piece of jigsaw and new prospects calling out of the blue wanting to see us because their friend told them about the jigsaw they should be buying!

CHAPTER 4

THE BUSINESS PLAN

Now we have seen how to generate a continuous stream of prospects, we need to make sure our business is sound. This is so that we do not become part of the statistics which say that two out of every three new businesses fail in the first three years and that we have a track to run on. It is no good making a great effort to win new clients and then find that we cannot keep them because our business does not run smoothly. Measurements of vital statistics are critical in any business and even more so in financial services. If we don't know where we are, in terms of sales, cash flow, income, expenditure and so on, we can't tell where we are going and we won't know if we are improving.

I wrote earlier that despite being treated awfully I was excited at being one of the few selected to be taken on as a new recruit as a financial adviser. I believe my employment was due in part to the fact that I had prepared a comprehensive business plan.

Even at the outset I had started practicing habits that would stand me in good stead later on. I bought and read a guide on how to write a business plan. Thanks to my background I was able to make it look visually attractive, but it was the content that swung it. My prospective employers could see that I had put a great deal of thought and effort into it and that I had commitment. I could see that if I carried out my plan, success was just around the corner!

A business plan should be for the user to work from, not just to impress a bank manager. A business plan takes at least a full day to devise, maybe longer and to do it properly we need to be armed with all the vital statistics we need. The numbers need to be accurate and detailed. This can often be a chore for many advisers as we can sometimes get carried away with the broad concepts and just want to get on with the client advising. To build a successful business the financial foundations should be set firmly in place. I wish I knew then all that I know now as it would have saved much financial woe, conversations with bank managers and money paid in overdraft fees.

A complete business plan will also take into account non-financial aspects, such as our goals for the business and the material things we would like to acquire.

This chapter will deal with just the time and money planning but for further information on the creation of business plans or goal setting, see Appendix B and Chapter 11 respectively.

It is imperative that we track our sales figures, more on this in Chapter 7, but equally important that we track our business expenses. The train fare here, some petrol there, through to the cost of printing a client magazine or staff wages, they all add up.

I recommend listing all your expenses under a number of headings. Of course, keep track of annual costs but for immediate understanding a monthly reconciliation is imperative. Keep fixed costs and variable costs separately. You may also want to factor in a multiplier if you have numerous advisers in your team or practice. This is because it is often the case that with the addition of another member to your team the fixed costs remain static but the variable costs will rise. For example, by taking on a paraplanner, the rent and photocopier lease payments will remain the same but telephone bills and paper usage will increase. Another big expenditure is tax. Always incorporate this when planning staff salaries or put sums aside if you are self-employed.

Remember to log marketing costs and regulatory fees. There are a number listed in my example but I'm sure you can think of your own. Remember this plan is for your use, so it doesn't have to adhere to accounting standards or be expensively bound. It should simply make sure that the information you need is at your fingertips to ensure that you are profitable. Remember to visit it often and update it when required. We wouldn't advise clients to invest in a company that had no financial plan or did not know what its income and expenditure was, so we shouldn't be that company ourselves!

We will see in later chapters how to merge this information with our vital business statistics so that we know the exact level of activity that we need in order to achieve our targets.

Part of the business plan should be to map out the year ahead. Take a full year planner and start with the most important item – You. Block out on the planner all the holidays you plan in the year as well as any other free time, such as public holidays and weekends. Then mark in any known dates that will keep you from seeing clients, such as conferences. What is left is the total amount of work days you have to achieve your aims.

If you have 200 days available to work and a target of £100,000 it is easy to see that you will need to generate an average of at least £500 per day to hit your target.

Having planned out your year and determined how many days you have available you now need to plan your days to make sure you hit your target. That is where The Success Plan comes in.

It is what you do with each and every day that will determine your success Whether you have succeeded or failed should not be a judgement made at midnight on December 31 each year but when you leave the office each evening.

In Chapter 2, I introduced the idea of the sales circle.

In the next few chapters we will go through the sales circle in detail and also 'The Success Plan'. The Success Plan is a one-page system to track activity and production and show how to increase success in all areas of your life, as well as multiply production.

SECTION 2

THE SUCCESS PLAN

CHAPTER 5

THE SUCCESS PLAN – AN OVERVIEW

The question is: As advisers, what are we worth?

Or to put it another way, if commission were abolished and we had to charge an hourly rate, what would it be? Write your own figure down in the space on the following page (Diagram 5.1).

I am going to summarise the seven key aims of the Success Plan that we will cover in the next few chapters. By the end of Chapter 7 we will know how to guarantee success every day, month and year by having a powerful set of daily goals and targets.

What Are We Worth?

If commission were abolished what would you charge as an hourly rate?

?________ Per hour

Diagram 5.1 – Hourly Rate

First off, we will learn the formula to calculate our true hourly worth and we'll see how to massively amplify it. Then we will discover ways to multiply the high value face-to-face time with clients, referrals obtained and personal or family time. We will find out how to decrease the time we spend in administration, how to automate the prospecting process and how to eradicate travel. I call all of the above, The Success Plan, and we are going to see how to operate 'The Success Plan' by using just one sheet of paper. It will operate alongside or in place of our current diary system and it is compatible with any way of operating, tied or independent, UK, US or overseas, just started or experienced adviser. Once the procedures are in place, and we will see them all in the next few chapters, it takes just 5 to 10 minutes per day thereafter to maintain, with maybe 30 minutes once a month to reflect and plan.

To determine what the average hourly rate would be, I carried out a poll amongst financial advisers, both tied and independent, at a number of the LIA regional meetings that I spoke at whilst writing this book (2001-2002). The average figure was £150 per hour with most answers between £100-£200. However, these were often guesses at best, so I came up with a formula to enable anyone to calculate their true hourly worth. Don't worry, the formula is as simple as A B C and is printed on the following page (Diagram 5.2) along with some sample figures.

We simply take our annual production, either historical (last year) or this year's target, it's up to us and write that in box A. For the example I've chosen annual production of £80,000 as a reasonable amount but not too close to the magic £100,000 figure that so many of us strive to achieve.

Then we write in box B1 the hours per day that we work. The example shows eight although industry records show many advisers work a lot longer day than that.

Finally, we fill in box B2 with the number of days per year worked. The example is 200, or putting it another way, about 40 weeks, which is probably about right for someone who never works weekends, never works on public holidays, attends the main national and international MDRT conference and one other convention, takes seven weeks holidays and is never ill! In other words, a very idealistic year and one that many of us probably can only dream of realising.

Now multiply box B1 by box B2 to calculate how many hours a year we work and write it in box C. Lastly, divide the annual production, A by the figure in C. That is our hourly chargeable rate. In the example it works out at £50 per hour.

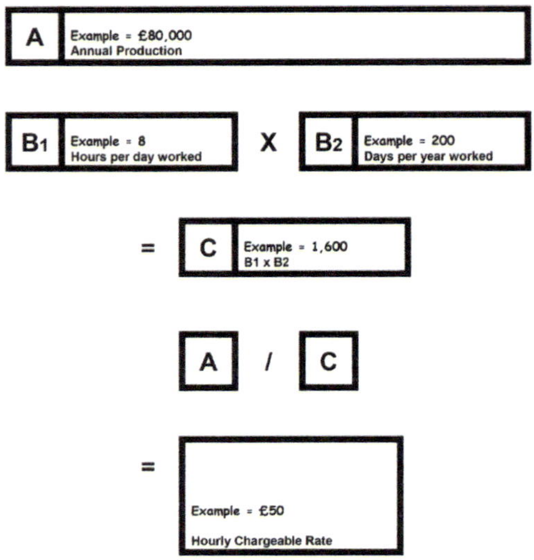

Diagram 5.2 – Hourly Rate Formula

Diagram 5.3 is a table showing how monthly or annual production translates to hourly rates.

Annual Production	Monthly Production	Days Worked	True Hourly Rate (8 hrs per day, 1600 hrs per annum)
25000	2083.33	200	15.63
50000	4166.67	200	31.25
63000	5250.00	200	39.38
80000	**6666.67**	**200**	**50.00**
100000	8333.33	200	62.50
150000	12500.00	200	93.75
160000	**13333.33**	**200**	**100.00**
189000	15750.00	200	118.13
240000	**20000.00**	**200**	**150.00**
250000	20833.33	200	156.25
320000	26666.67	200	200.00
350000	29166.67	200	218.75
378000	31500.00	200	236.25
400000	**33333.33**	**200**	**250.00**

Diagram 5.3 – Hourly Rates

The figure of £50 an hour in our example was very much at the lower end of the figures that most advisers would consider charging. And you can see that the example was pretty generous. Anyone achieving production of £80,000 a year but working longer hours, or taking less holiday, being ill once in a while, or working the odd weekend would have a lower figure than £50 per hour. For many advisers this exercise is very scary because we tend to just keep on working as we get work in and letting the year drift past. I am sure there may even be a few people reading this who don't even know how many days they work each year. And there may even be a few who struggle to remember the last time they worked an 8-hour day or had more than one week off.

What usually happens when people see this table is that those of us who consider we would charge £100 per hour, look across and realise we are producing nowhere near £13,000 each and every month. And those who consider they would charge nearer £200 per hour aren't quite at £250,000 yet.

Take a look at one more table, shown in Diagram 5.4. Some would say that this is a more realistic table than the last one because the example shows someone who works a 14 hour day, one day every other weekend, works on a few public holidays and takes just 2 weeks holiday per year. In other words, 275 days or 3850 hours per year. Or going by industry records, more typical of most financial advisers.

If we relate these hours back to our example of £80,000 per year we can see the hourly rate reduced from £50 per hour to just over £20 per hour.

Annual Production	Monthly Production	Days Worked	True Hourly Rate (14 hrs per day, 3850 hrs per annum)
25000	2083.33	275	6.49
50000	4166.67	275	12.99
63000	5250.00	275	16.36
80000	6666.67	275	20.78
100000	8333.33	275	25.97
150000	12500.00	275	38.96
160000	13333.33	275	41.56
189000	15750.00	275	49.09
240000	20000.00	275	62.34
250000	20833.33	275	64.94
320000	26666.67	275	83.12
350000	29166.67	275	90.91
378000	31500.00	275	98.18
400000	33333.33	275	103.90

Diagram 5.4 – Hourly Rates

What can be seen from this diagram is that anyone working that hard and considering their worth at £100 per hour should be MDRT Top of the Table (see Appendix A). A more usual response is a funny feeling in the stomach as we realise we are unaware of our true worth and that we have been grossly undercharging our clients for the hard work we put in on their behalf. We can also see that we have been working as a financial services professional yet earning the hourly rate of an administrative clerk.

How many of us reading this are working more than 8 hours per day or 200 days a year and not reaching the production we should be? – WHY?

To discover this, we need to analyse exactly what we are doing every single day. The key to 'The Success Plan' is having daily goals and targets and meeting them. There is an old question which goes "How do you eat an elephant?" The answer is, of course, "In small pieces"

And that is what we have to do with our goals and targets. Break them down into small pieces.

With £100,000 as an annual target and working 48 weeks per year, this leaves a weekly target of £2,083. If we have an average case size of £520, this means four sales. Assume we have eight client meetings to close the four required cases at 1 hour per meeting. This equals just 8 hours from the 40 available in the week in front of clients.

I'm going to ask the question posed at the beginning of the chapter again: As advisers, what are we worth?

When face to face with clients we are worth £260 per hour – that is £2,083 weekly production divided by 8 hours with clients.

The rest of the time we are doing £26, £16 or even £6 per hour work. When we are not seeing clients we are doing work that someone else could do for a lot less than we charge.

Would you rather be earning £260 or £26 per hour?
Question: How do we move from £26 per hour to £260 per hour?
Answer: Stop doing £26 per hour tasks.

To determine when we are doing £260 per hour tasks and when we are doing £26 per hour tasks we must track our time carefully. This is where the main body of The Success Plan comes into play.

The following exercise will show us how to massively increase our productivity. First, we must split our diary into months, then weeks, then days, then hours, then 15 minute segments. As I said, many of us may already have a diary set out like this – that is fine. If not, use The Success Planner page (see Diagram 5.5). I have used 15-minute segments but many are adopting the system used by most legal practices of 6-minute segments. My experience shows that 15-minute segments are fine for tracking personal sales and production figures but if you will also be using the daily planner to track case work for fee charging (see Chapter 8) I suggest 6-minute segments give greater accuracy.

A very useful and productive tip to automatically increase our production by 8%, or to take an extra 4 weeks holiday per year, is to split our year into 13 'months' of 4 weeks each (52 weeks) instead of 12 months (52 weeks). Do this with your personal records even if your host company does not work this way.

Diagram 5.6 shows a typical diary for an adviser.

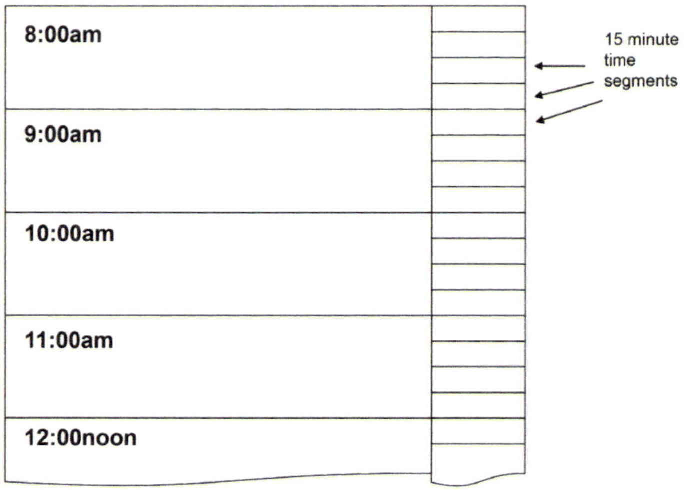

Diagram 5.5 – 15 Minute Segments

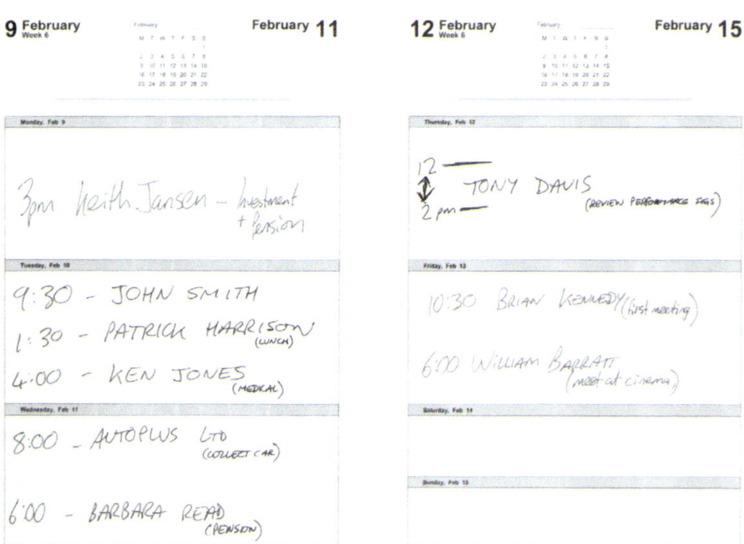

Diagram 5.6 – Old Diary

The adviser has appointments on quite a few days over the week and to the casual observer it looks like quite a full diary, perhaps that of a very busy person. But on closer inspection we can see that a few of the entries that look like appointments are actually something else, such as a lunch date with a friend, a review meeting with a manager, picking up the car from the garage and so on. And the real appointments that have been written in are in unusually large writing, giving the effect of a full day but in reality, only taking an hour or two. In actual fact, this is my old diary!

Shown in Diagram 5.7 below is a day from my current diary using the success plan principles. I'd like to point out two things. The first is that every hour is broken into 15-minute segments, from 8:00am through to 6:00pm. The second is that some of the segments are shaded. These principles and others are explained in the next chapter.

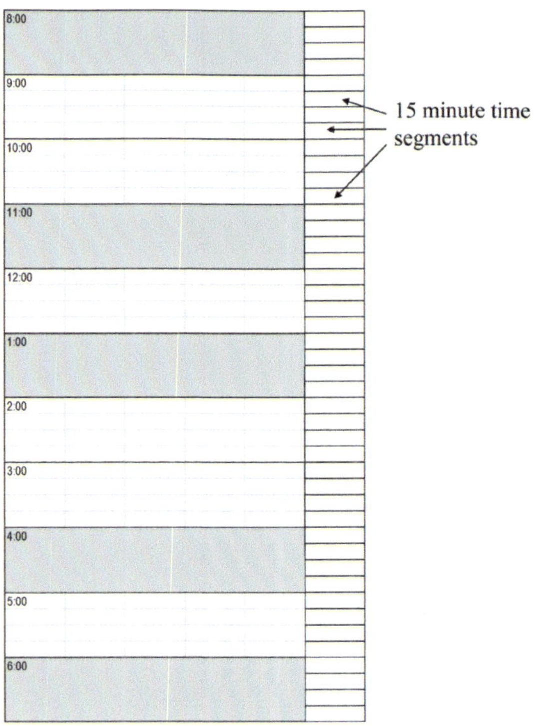

Diagram 5.7 – 15 Minute Segments Plus Shading

CHAPTER 6

THE SUCCESS PLAN – COLOURS

Let's get down to the 15-minute segments (see Appendix A-2). This is crucial to our success. We need to go out and buy five new pens. One Red, one Blue, one Green, one Yellow and one Black (see Diagram 6.1).

RED	Face to face
BLUE	Prospecting
GREEN	Personal
YELLOW	Travel
BLACK	Admin

Diagram 6.1 – The Colours

Even if we already own five pens of these colours we need to go and buy some more. I'll explain why. As each 15-minute segment of the day passes, we colour in a segment on our Success Plan.

Red – if we were face to face with clients

Blue – if we were prospecting

Green – if it was personal or family time

Yellow – if we were travelling

Black – if we were involved in administration

The reason we must purchase five new pens, is if we are anything like I was five years ago, the black one will run out long before the others! And the yellow one didn't last long ... and I've still got my original red one – no just kidding!

At the end of each day, we spend 5 minutes calculating the percentage of time we spent in each colour.

There is part of a typical day coloured in Diagram 6.2.

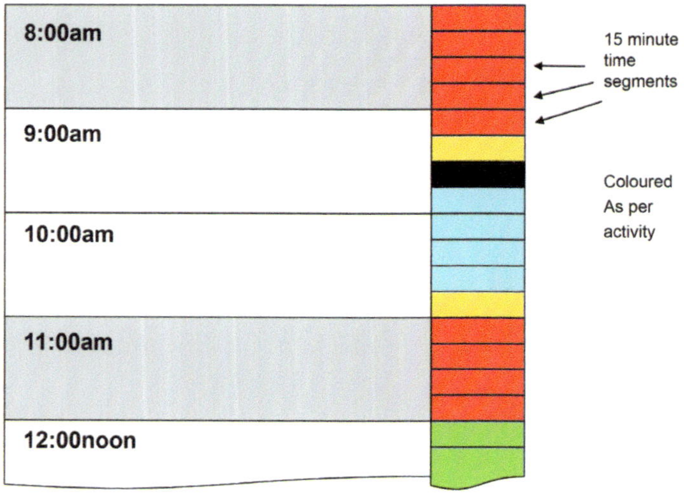

Diagram 6.2 – 15 Minute Segments – Coloured

I am certain that for many reading this, having completed the planner for at least four weeks, we will find more than 50% of our diary is coloured black, no more than 20% is red and that there is little green and too much yellow.

How do we increase the red (£260ph) and the green (personal time) and decrease the blue, yellow and most importantly black?

6.1 Red – face-to-face

We'll address each colour in turn. First and most importantly is how to increase the red time. We are going to see how to increase the amount of time we spend with clients and how to obtain an extra day each week. Look at Diagram 5.7 again and notice the shaded areas.

These are the meeting slots. These are the only times that we can see people on that day. What we have done is to goal set our diary. This means things will happen!

First, we trigger the goal setting mechanism in our heads to start filling the gaps. By having specific slots to fill we can't suddenly start writing in twice our normal size to fill up the day and kid ourselves we are busy. Immediately we find the capacity for an extraordinary number of meetings. When we call a client to book a meeting, suddenly we are in control, not them. No more meetings at 8pm in the evening. There is no slot available. No more meetings at 12 noon, meaning we can only see one person at lunchtime or we have to eat at strange times. The slots are 11am or 1pm. Period. You may be thinking 'surely it can't be this easy' or 'that won't work for me, I have to be flexible for my clients' or 'some of my clients can only see me in the evening'.

"Is it that easy?" – Yes it is! However, I would say that if we are going to drastically change our working habits we should let our clients know. As an example, when my wife and I discovered she was pregnant I decided that when my son was born, I would only work evenings one night a week. Up until that point I was working nearly every evening. I wrote to my clients, explaining what I would be doing and why I would be doing it and asking that if they did need an evening appointment, to book it well in advance. The response from clients was overwhelmingly positive. Now I work an occasional evening and my production has increased, not decreased.

"It won't work for me, I have to be flexible" – I urge you to try it. I thought it wouldn't work for me. But don't just take my word for it. For further proof, look to other professions, such as legal or medical.

If we want to see a lawyer, we call up and make an appointment. If the lawyer we want can't see us for three days, what do we do? Decide we'll not bother with the litigation or do it ourselves? Of course not, we see him as soon as HE is able to fit us in. If we need an operation the same rules apply. We need a specialist surgeon so we get a slot in his diary. We are no different. We are financial specialists, we are professionals. If a prospect wants to see us enough they'll find a slot. If they don't want to see us that much, the harsh reality is they probably weren't a very good client or prospect in the first place. Yes, we might lose a few clients but if we gain our evenings back with our family or find time to play sport or whatever it is we want to do then it is a small price to pay.

"My clients will only see me in the evening, or at the weekend" – Given the choice, many clients don't want to talk about life insurance, or investments, or retirement planning at all, let alone in the evening or Saturday morning. As before, if they are serious, they will find time during the day. No matter how busy they are, I am sure they take time out to go to the dentist, to take the dog to the vet or the car to the garage. They just need to do the same for their finances.

Diagram 6.3 shows my Success Planner for a week. Notice how I have seventeen possible meeting slots and yet I work no weekends, I arrive at work at 10am on a Monday, I have time available for lunch each day, I never start before 8am, I leave every day at 6pm except when I work late until 7pm on a Tuesday or leave early at 4pm on a Friday. Whatever time slot someone wants, it is available somewhere in the week, from 8am to 6pm. There really is no excuse for not finding a mutually convenient time in the next four weeks.

I still work hard but including lunch my week has potential for 45 hours. More than your average Joe, but a lot less than your average financial adviser. Do I have seventeen meetings each and every week? No. But I have a lot more than when I just scribbled in my diary and I work a lot less hours. It is a focused week!

Another way to increase the red time is to decrease the time spent face to face with clients doing mundane tasks, such as introducing ourselves and our credentials and 'hard' fact finding. As I have already stated I am not so naïve as to think we can conduct business without seeing someone and I am not suggesting it. There will always be a requirement to meet and it is only when face to face that we as advisers can really get a grip on the 'soft facts', the hopes, dreams and desires of our clients. But think how much time we would save if we didn't have to spend the first meeting chit chatting and gathering details on the existing situation. If all that were already done, we could spend the first meeting building rapport and doing what we get paid for – solving financial problems.

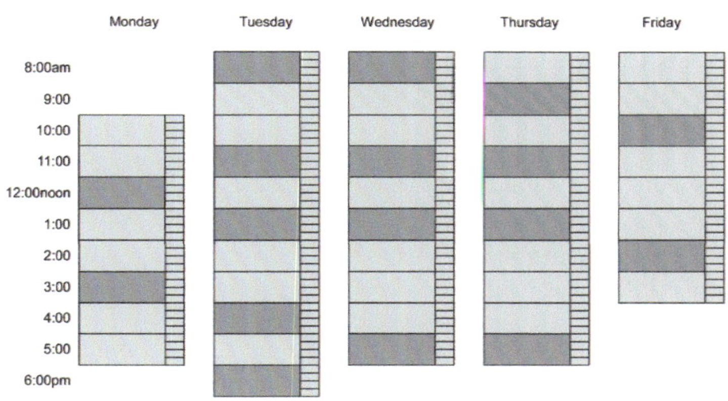

Diagram 6.3 – The Success Plan – Week

In order to achieve this, we can do two things. First, have a document prepared that introduces our company and us as individuals. On one side it could contain details about our company or agency, such as when it was established, funds under management, product specialisation and so on. On the other side can be a picture of us, our credentials, and testimonials from existing clients.

Independent testimonials from a third party are incredibly powerful and should not be underestimated or under used. If we have none, we should make it our number one task to ask our clients for favourable quotations that we can use.

Secondly, send our fact-finding document, or a smaller version of it, in advance of the meeting (see Appendix A-3). This can be done by post, fax or even electronically via email or our website. Explain in a covering letter that we need this completed in advance so that the time spent together is valuable particularly for the client. Also ask for any documentation such as copies of wage slips, company benefits or existing policies. If our company or agency has a complicated form that would baffle a client or we do it all on computer, design your own mini-questionnaire, asking the questions needed.

When we then meet the client, we can use the meeting time far more effectively and efficiently. The same principle can be applied to completing the business. Just send out the forms for signing clearly marked, with known details such as name, address, premiums and so on pre-populated. Include a checklist for completion and a telephone helpline number in case of difficulty.

As before, if a client wants the plan, they will complete the forms. If you feel your clients may not complete the form, my feeling is that in most cases they don't want, or need the plan enough.

Consider a typical adviser. They usually take three meetings from start to finish for a new client to complete a new piece of business. Meeting one is the introduction, lots of time spent getting to know each other and completing the fact-find. Meeting two, the adviser returns to explain his recommendations and gain agreement from the client. Meeting three is the final signing. In between there are probably quite a few telephone calls, chasing documentation, clarifying detail and so on. Applying what we have just seen takes away the first and last meeting and most of the admin chasing.

The client sees who we are and what we do from the brochure and provides all the necessary data. We meet and present our case. Then we send everything for signing having made any changes requested. It has taken one hour instead of three, and if we include travel time, say thirty minutes each way, each meeting, we have taken two hours instead of six.

Do this three times a week and we have saved twelve hours – a whole day. Who would like an extra day each week? There you go, have that one on me!

6.2 Yellow – travel

Talking of travelling, let's move onto Yellow and how it can be decreased. We will now see how to eradicate travel or at least take it to an absolute minimum.

Number one is to work 'in-house'. Get the clients to come to us. It really is that simple, just ask!

But what if they ask why they should visit us now when we were always happy to visit them in the past? Explain that financial services grows ever more complex and we need our research materials, computer systems and reference books to hand.

After all, what would we think of a dentist who came to our house at 7:30 in the evening with a bag full of drills and asked us to lean back in our easy chair, or a lawyer who called round at the weekend? As with our earlier comparison if we want to be seen as professionals we must act as professionals. We often hear the excuse that we do not have an office to use. The long-term answer is to get one! But I am aware that this takes time, cash and planning. So, let's agree to put that on our goal list and in our business plans (we should all have a business plan – if not read Chapter 4!) and come up with some more immediate solutions.

What if we don't have an office? Meet in the lobby or restaurant of a smart local hotel. Nil cost. Many hotels and even motorway service stations now have dedicated rooms that can be hired by the day or hour. What if we don't have a smart hotel near us?

Hire a room in a set of serviced offices for the day. They will have wonderful reception staff, top quality furniture and office facilities and food and drinks can be supplied at a nominal cost. There are a number of companies running these facilities all over the world. By doing a little groundwork in advance you can usually find an operator with premises in all the areas you need, giving you office space right across a city or country at negligible cost.

What if there are no serviced offices? Approach a local fellow professional, such as an accountant or lawyer and hire a meeting room from them. It is a win-win situation as if chosen carefully their services will doubtless be of use to us and our clients and vice versa. I'll bet that after a few sessions we start to pick up client casework from them that more than pays for the hire of the room! Profitable!

Another way to reduce travel time is to stop commuting and work nearer home. Let's use myself as an example again. I used to work in the heart of London. I don't live that far out but public transport is not so good these days and traffic congestion is everywhere. It usually took three hours travel per day. Instead I rented an office ten minutes walk from my house. It saves me hours of time each week as well as saving money and commuter frustration.

For the same reasons, clients love to visit me! We have reached a point where many clients are not impressed by big flashy offices in the centre of the city. Firstly, they are difficult to get to and often clients end up looking at our marble reception and vast glass atrium thinking that this is where all their money is going! Clients love to take time out to visit nice places so make sure your office, if based locally, has basic facilities available such as parking or easy access by public transport. This makes the process of visiting you a pleasure, not a chore. I even know of one financial adviser who has his client's cars washed whilst the meeting is in progress (see Appendix A-4). Make the place a little homely with fresh flowers, ensure it is neat, tidy and presentable, not unkempt with piles of paper on the floor. In short, the kind of place that you would like to visit. We can often lose sight of this fact as our familiarity with the surroundings can conceal the true state of the office.

If we have just eight meetings a week, with thirty minutes travel time to and from each one, we gain an extra eight hours per week by not travelling. We have just gained an extra 20% time each week.

But I accept that sometimes it is just not possible to see everyone in our office, for example if we are in the corporate market it is hard to get a team of three owner/shareholders out together.

If we do have to go out, use the diary goal setting principle. I have split my diary into three sections. Tuesdays are for clients based in the centre of the city, Wednesdays are for the west of town and Thursdays are for the financial or docklands areas. If I have to travel outside the city I go on a Monday. Fridays are always spent in the office. My clients know this. So, if someone from the west calls, they can have their pick of the times on a Wednesday. By grouping clients together like this I cut down on travel. I never have to go all the way across town and back again in one day. My meetings are localised. This also cuts down on costs, such as public transport, or petrol and parking.

6.3 Green – personal

Continuing with the goal setting diary principle brings us to green time, the personal or family time. Most of us will be in the position of wanting to increase this. Take exactly the same approach as before.

Book it in your diary and treat it just like any other appointment. Well almost like any other appointment! We should treat it even more importantly than client time. Just as I did when my son was born, if scheduling more green time would have a dramatic effect on our current working patterns, we should let our clients know.

If we think we would like more time at the gym, the golf club, or at a spa, then we need to book an appointment with ourselves. If we have an event for our children coming up, such as an important sports game or the school play, book it in the diary. I guarantee that if a client requests a meeting and we explain that we can't make that time because our child is receiving a prize and we are attending the ceremony, they won't mind. Especially, if we are able to offer a whole host of alternative slots from our schedule straight away.

And I would say that if any client refused me business because I gave the reason I had an important family matter to attend to that I wouldn't want to deal with them anyway. It is all about priorities.

Many of us may be sitting there thinking that we would like to give ourselves and our family more time but just don't see how we can. If the reason really is just time, then sit down and work through all the concepts in the Success Plan, calculate where you could save just one hour and immediately allocate it as green time. It may be thirty minutes saved by not travelling once a week and thirty minutes by sending out forms for signing once, but you will be able to find savings.

However, if our heart is willing but the head seems to be stopping us, or in other words we know it is a good idea but there is always too much 'stuff' undone, the answer may be to write a list of all the things we would do if we had more green time. Look at Diagram 6.4.

Write the green time events down the left. Write in one column what the consequences will be of taking that time, the positive factors and in the next column write the consequences of not taking the time, the negative factors. By doing this you should find at least one compelling reason to put your family or yourself first.

Green Time Personal / Family Event	+ Positives From taking the time	- Negatives From NOT taking the time
GO TO GYM 3 TIMES PER WEEK	1. FEEL BETTER & LOOK BETTER 2. BUY NEW WARDROBE! 3. WILL HIT WEIGHT LOSS TARGET	1. NOT SLEEPING PROPERLY 2. OUT OF BREATH STAIR-CLIMBING 3. KIDS BEAT ME AT TENNIS!
HOME ON TIME TO READ BEDTIME STORY TO BABY AND EAT DINNER WITH WIFE	1. SPEND QUALITY TIME WITH CHILDREN AND WIFE 2. TIME TO RELAX BEFORE BED, INSTEAD OF HOME, EAT, SLEEP, OUT AGAIN 3.	1. MISSING CHILDREN GROWING UP 2. ..... 3. .....

Diagram 6.4 – Green Reasons

I used to have a problem in my own mind with green time. It seemed I would let myself have green time only when I felt I had deserved it. Therefore, I would tend to work and work and work almost to the point of breakdown before allowing myself a day off, and by that time I would usually be ill from my exertions anyway. It was as if I were trying to move a boulder from A to B by pushing it up a hill and as I got further up the hill, gravity would be working harder against me until I finally heaved it to the top and pushed it over the cliff. (See Diagram 6.5.) At that point I would finally rest or more likely collapse.

Then I realised I was doing things the wrong way around. (See Diagram 6.6.) It shows that the easiest way to get the boulder from A to B is to be completely rested FIRST. Then it is a simple matter to roll the boulder down the hill. As long as some effort is applied on the way down it is relatively easy to keep the momentum going and push it up the next hill.

Diagram 6.5 – Boulders

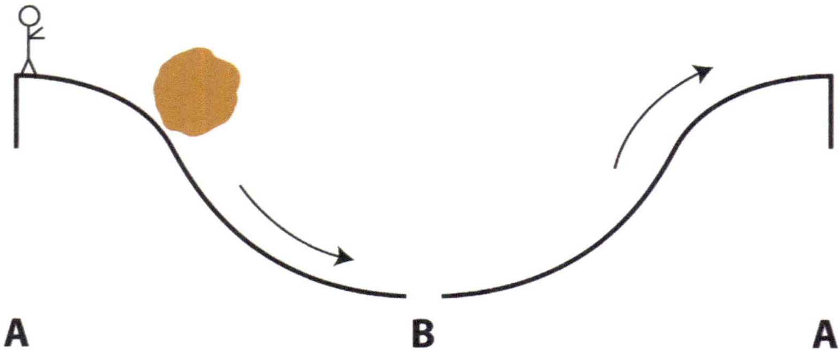

Diagram 6.6 – Boulders

These two simple drawings changed my life. But there was still something else missing. For many of us, the main thing stopping us going home on time, taking weekends off, or getting to the school play is the sheer volume of paperwork we have to deal with. Admin!

6.4 Black – administration

I wrote earlier of the need to go out and purchase five new, coloured pens. For most of us here, the reason for this becomes obvious as soon as we start filling in the Success Plan.

The black pen takes a heck of a beating. If we really take the Success Plan to heart we will come to hate our black pen. If we are anything like most advisers, and certainly like you if you have read this far, we will have a high degree of professional pride and a high degree of motivation.

The trouble is, sometimes we get distracted or have to go into firefighting mode, bouncing from one crisis to another. Unchecked, this turns into days and even weeks where we recall being very busy and having no time to ourselves, no new production on our figures and nothing ticked off the to-do list on Friday that was already there at the start of the week.

We can all guess why we have so much black on our Success Planners. It is the increased regulatory burden that we are all facing.

The extra paperwork needed to substantiate our recommendations, the extra documentation needed for money laundering and client verification, the increased demands for great customer service, the ever increasing number of applications receiving a rating and taking extra work to get a case on risk. I could go on and on. The trouble is that this is all £26 per hour work, not £260 per hour work. Remember that? The answer is to delegate.

The very fact that you are reading this demonstrates that you have ability and the desire to succeed. But what we mustn't get confused about is that we should think we are the only person who can do our job. There are aspects of our job that we may well be good at but the fact remains we should only be doing the elements of our work that only we can do. The other aspects, all the factors that we call 'admin' we should not be doing. We have all heard the top producers stand on main platforms at conferences and read books that tell us to delegate.

But have we all done it? Do we all really believe it? Once again, rather than just tell you it is a good idea, I'm going to prove it and show you my own example and how it can work for you also.

As an example assume a salary for an assistant of £20,000. Divide this by 52 weeks and assume working 40 hours per week. This is just under £10 per hour. We, the advisers are worth £50, £100, £260 per hour, or more. Remember at the beginning of Chapter 6.1 we discussed this. These admin tasks cost £10 per hour to complete, or less. On our examples we have seen that every time we colour in a segment of our Success Plan in red we can generate hundreds of £ per hour.

Every time we use the black pen we are working at £10 per hour. If we want further motivation, take a sticker, write £10 per hour on it and stick it on our black pen as a reminder each time we pick it up!

£10 per hour, pay someone else to do it! A typical adviser will spend 50% of his or her time on admin tasks. Think how much time we would free-up for face to face time with clients, time with our family or for our own interests, if we didn't have so much admin work. How many evenings would we gain by not having to work late? How many weekends could we reclaim? How much would our quality of life improve? How does this fit in with our typical adviser?

Remember the average case size is just £500. With the salary example we just looked at we would have to complete less than one extra case per week. Of course we will still need to do some admin, that is inescapable. But assuming as an adviser that we are working a 50-hour week and 50% of that time is taken with admin here is what happens when we delegate just half of it, or 25% of the total admin. 12 hours are freed up. Could we write an extra case, or commission of £500 given another 12 hours, a whole day? For most advisers, the answer is a resounding YES!

Consider the adviser who decides to implement some of the ideas from the Success Plan discussed so far. For example, having more meetings each week by goal setting the diary, leaving the office on time as there are no evening slots, sending out a fact find for 'hard fact' completion before the meeting, travelling locally on specific days and delegating most of the £10 per hour admin. It is not difficult to imagine being able to complete a few thousand £ per week of extra production, whether through concentrating on a few bigger cases or just more cases of the £500 average.

By delegating and writing just four extra cases a month we can easily double our production. Taking out the salary of £20,000 this still leaves extra profit and all that in addition to the extra green personal time gained.

My own business backs up these figures. In the last two years, since implementing these concepts my production has doubled. In addition, I now work an average 40-hour week instead of the 70 hours that was usual before working in this fashion.

I would add that finding the right person to delegate to is crucial and I would urge you to consider the use of a high-quality recruitment consultant and the latest in personal profiling tests before employing anyone. At the very least read a book or attend a seminar on how to hire the right person. I went through four assistants in four years in my search for the right person and now I am in the situation whereby if my assistant left I would struggle to run the business on my own. Without doubt the biggest factor in doubling my production was the addition of a top-class assistant to my business. In fact, many clients prefer to call and speak to my assistant for day-to-day tasks and this is how it should be. My clients know that my staff are of the highest quality and can be trusted to carry out their requests therefore I am left free to concentrate on tasks that require my ability (and fee). The fact is that my staff are actually better at carrying out the administrative tasks than I am!

There are many other tasks that can be delegated. I suggest you keep a piece of paper to hand for two to three weeks and write down everything you do, from opening the mail to seeing clients and everything in between (see Appendix A-5). Then look at the list and see if there is anything that would be economical to delegate. Combine your list with the output of your Success Planner. For example, you may find that a large portion of your time is spent driving from meeting to meeting. If you follow the success plan principle of 'localising' your meetings you may find it economical to hire a driver for the day. By having all your meetings geographically closer together the time that is spent in the car is minimised, leaving more time for meetings (more red time). I find that just one extra sale a day justifies the cost of the driver. Who should the driver be? You may have a local taxi firm that can take the work on. You might want to go all the way and hire a uniformed chauffeur from an executive hire company or you may even know someone locally who knows their way around and would be grateful for a little extra income a few days a week. But the efficiencies go further still. Instead of concentrating on the road you are free to make calls or catch up on reading, meaning yellow time is converted to blue or green time. Time and money you would normally have spent on parking are also diminished as you are simply dropped off and collected at leisure. And of course, the cost of the driver is tax deductible as a business expense!

Likewise, you can apply the principle to other areas of the business too, such as answering the phone (receptionist), file preparation and obtaining client quotations (paraplanner) or opening the post and ordering stationery (office manager). Log your activity and determine what you can effectively and economically delegate and watch your red time and profits soar.

6.5 Blue – prospecting with referrals

The only colour left is blue. The only way we can guarantee success is with a continuous stream of prospects. It is often said, "If you don't have any prospects, you don't have any prospects". Many would say that increasing blue, prospecting time, would be a good thing. And I used to agree. But having run The Success Plan for some time now I have come to the conclusion that blue time is also best delegated to someone else, our clients. There are a few exceptions and these are dealt with later but it is generally agreed that the most efficient way of obtaining new clients is by personal recommendation. Therefore, we should obtain referrals and let our clients do the prospecting for us. The referral obtaining process should be automatic. Especially as "How do we obtain more clients?" is one of the most repeated questions in our profession, especially for those just starting out or the younger ones amongst us. For those who have been in the industry a little longer, there is the recognition that new clients typically provide a higher average case size and are needed to keep the business fresh. Therefore, we all constantly strive to add to our client base.

I propose we change the question and ask ourselves, "how do we obtain more QUALITY clients?"

This chapter will show how to move your practice from traditional time consuming expensive prospecting that yields new clients of arbitrary value to prospecting that generates a constant stream of high quality referrals. As with everything in this book, this is not theory, this works and I will be giving practical examples.

Let us examine the classic way of obtaining referrals. There are two things we must be doing, before anything else.

Firstly:

- **we must create value and give service to our clients;**

and secondly:

- **we must ask!**

If we are not doing these two basics I guarantee we will not be getting referrals.

Now let's assume that everyone reading this is creating value and giving service and we'll assume that we all ask for referrals at point of sale, having built it into our presentation from the first meeting. If we are doing these two simple things we deserve referrals. If we are not doing the above, or do not think we deserve referrals we must ask ourselves why not? If we are hesitant to refer ourselves then there is something wrong!

We are told that referability depends upon four things:

1. Arrive on time
2. Do what you say
3. Finish what you start and
4. Say please and thank you. (See Appendix A-5.)

In addition, we should be technically competent in the products we advise on.

Here is where the majority of us face a challenge. We do practice the Referability Habits, we are technically competent, we do give great value to our clients. But if we provide great service to all clients, we obtain referrals from all clients. How many of us have had a call from a referral that goes something like this: “You don’t know me but John suggested I call you. He said you sold him a £50 a month rebated commission saving plan. Can you help me get one of those?”

I am sure we all appreciate the referral and it is nice to know our client recommended us but we won’t survive as a business for very long if we keep doing work without payment, even if it is referred.

Take a moment to consider your client base right now. It doesn’t matter if you only have two clients or two thousand clients. Picture in your mind your worst client. Consider the type of business that would be referred by your worst client. Now picture in your mind the type of business that would be referred by your best client. Is this starting to make sense? Can you see where we are going? If we give the same service to everyone we may get a referral from our top client but the danger is that we may get a referral from our worst client. And whichever one it is, we do the work!

Many of us will be familiar with the 80/20 rule, the so-called Pareto Principle. What follows is a slight variation on that rule. If we analyse the clients we sell to in one year, unless all our clients have identical incomes and occupations, this is what we will find. No matter how many people we sell to, 50% of our income will come from 20 clients. Note, it is twenty clients, not 20% of clients. If we sell to one hundred clients, 50% of our income will come from the top twenty clients. If we sell to two hundred clients, 50% of our income will come from the top twenty clients. If we sell to four hundred clients, 50% of our income will still come from the top twenty clients (see Appendix A-6).

The key message here is that in order to improve the quality of referrals obtained, the focus must be on the quality of service provided to quality clients.

Most of us will be familiar with goal setting. If not please read Chapter 11 and Appendix B and consider one of the titles listed there. What we are going to do is goal set our referrals. To do this we need to know who our top twenty clients are. Mine are defined as people that I get along with, those who are entrepreneurially minded, those who have great economic potential, who do business with me in more than one area of financial planning and therefore those who offer further opportunities for business in the future.

Take some time to list your top twenty clients. You can use the grid in Diagram 6.7. When I first carried out this exercise I only had fourteen people in my top twenty! There were only fourteen people who fitted my criteria, but that was OK as we are going to see now how to fill in the missing names. To the right of the names column are three referrals columns. These are what we need to fill. Take your pen and fill in the names of any referrals received from your top twenty clients. You may not be able to fill any gaps and you probably won't fill in more than half (see Appendix A-6).

No.	Client	Referral 1	Referral 2	Referral 3
1				
2				
3				
4				
5				
6				
7				
8				
9				
10				
11				
12				
13				
14				
15				
16				
17				
18				
19				
20				

Average case size from top 20 client =	
multiplied by	x
Number of gaps on your list	
equals	=
Potential production from top 20 referrals =	

Diagram 6.7 – Sixty Referrals

Even if we only have a few names, we can now see in front of us ways to take our business forward. What happens now is that the goal setting mechanism in our brain will start to help us to fill the gaps. We will have a natural desire to see them all filled.

If you do have three referrals from one client and they match your criteria, add them to the bottom of your list and start obtaining referrals again with the new name. This is a never ending, self-generating process.

As a very quick exercise, in the space at the bottom of Diagram 6.7, write down the average case size you think you would obtain from one of your top twenty clients. Remember these are the best of the best. Is it £500, £1,000, £5,000, £10,000? Now count the referral gaps on your own handout and write it in the space provided. Now multiply the average case size by the number of gaps. Pretty exciting figures, huh? We are starting to see how focusing our efforts like a laser on our top clients rather than scattering our efforts across our whole client base can reap rewards.

It is important to place these lists where we can see them, for example on the wall over our desks or in our diary where our subconscious mind is reminded every day of the task in hand.

As an example, when I did this exercise, here is what happened. I called one of my clients and said “Hi Fred, it’s Ian Green”. Fred said “I’m glad you rang, I’ve been meaning to call you”. (Has that ever happened to you?) “Can you come over to the office sometime, I’ve told two of my associates about the estate planning we carried out and they want the same plan that I have”. Now remember, this was one of my biggest clients, and I’ve just been referred the same thing twice over. “Sure, Fred” I said (kicking myself for not having asked earlier – remember the basics – ASK!) and we booked a time for me to see his colleagues. “Now what was it you wanted Ian?”. “Fred, could you give me the name and telephone number of your lawyer”. “Sure Ian, is there anything wrong?”. “Nothing wrong Fred, but as we were successful with your planning I thought he may have similar clients that I could help in the same way”.

To cut a long story short, the end result was that Fred was delighted to be able to help me and actually contacted his lawyer to tell him I would be ringing. When I called the lawyer he was also glad that I called as he had been looking for a trustworthy financial planner. Since then we have worked together on a number of projects that have generated a substantial amount of business for us both. That one ‘phone call, combined with the basics, has been responsible for a large amount of income. Go on try it, it works!

Here is an example of focused marketing that can help generate referrals.

I'm sure you have heard that we should keep in touch with our clients by sending out a newsletter? How many of us actually do keep in touch with our clients by sending out a newsletter? Look at what happens when we focus our time, effort and own business investment:

Here is an example of what many of us are already doing:

Client Contact (for example a client magazine)

Clients = all 500 (500 clients = typical adviser active client base)
Item cost (inc printing and postage) = £2
Total cost = £1,000

How about this as an alternative?

Here is an example of what we should be doing:

Quality Client Contact (example business tape program)
Clients = top 20
Item cost = £50 (including postage)
Total cost = £1,000

Think of the impression you will make on your top twenty clients by presenting them with a £50 tape program – if you are stuck for ideas there are many excellent tapes, videos and books available from most business bookshops. If we received something from a supplier, which would we prefer? How would we feel if we received a £50 value gift with a covering letter informing us we were one of the suppliers top twenty clients? Pretty special, huh? We have started to tip the scales in favour of obtaining a referral from our best clients and not from our worst.

In the example we had a total marketing cost of £1,000. Is this good or bad, too much or too little? There is no right or wrong answer as it depends on the profit we will make from a client and how many clients the exercise will generate. There is a whole chapter on business and client data tracking later in the book.

Here are the keys to our marketing strategy:

1. Knowing the cost of acquiring a new client; and
2. Knowing our average case size.

We must know these figures for our own businesses before we can progress. Take a look at Chapter 7 for the full breakdown but essentially to calculate your profit per client, take the gross production generated and take away costs (such as agency fees, staff costs, rent, etc). I work on a net profit of between 10% and 20%, so for brevity let us call it an average of 15%.

My average case size from my top twenty clients is £4,161. My average case size from my whole client base is £1,905. The cases from the top twenty are, on average, over twice as large as the rest. Notice these cases are not huge, but they are not small neither. I am not one of the superstars of our industry who complete giant cases each day. I just work this system. The important thing is that my average is going up each year. I know that my average top twenty cases will generate £4,000 and I will make a profit of £600. I can comfortably spend £300 on the client to obtain more business and still make a profit. By contrast, profit on an average client taken from the whole client base is £285 in total, less than the marketing budget for a top twenty client.

We must ensure we carry out the exercise of calculating our client profitability. Then we must calculate our average case size for our whole client base and compare it to the average case size obtained from our top twenty clients.

Once we know our average case size and profit per case, then we can structure our marketing budget and activity to fit. I will be giving working examples of referral marketing ideas later in the chapter.

To confirm, we need to improve and focus on the service and relationships we have with our existing top twenty clients. They will refer us to further excellent prospects. Do not take referrals from anyone else. I imagine that at this stage some readers may be thinking, "I can't afford to do that". Remember the figures we have just looked at. The truth is, we can't afford not to do it. In the following example I'm going to prove it.

We are now going to run through a typical example of an adviser with five hundred active client files who provides an adequate level of service to all their clients and practises a mixture of prospecting methods. This adviser, like most readers I'm sure, always shows up on time, knows the technical stuff and has great relationships with clients.

This adviser receives eight referrals per month, which is two a week and these come from clients telephoning in, social prospecting and a regular mailing. Once a month a seminar is held which also generates eight cold prospects. Of the sixteen names collected each month the majority are OK, there are usually a few 'time wasters' and every so often the adviser strikes it lucky with a large case. On average, 75% of the referrals and 50% of the cold prospects become clients. This is ten new clients per month, or one hundred and twenty per annum.

The average case size is £600, which means production of £72,000 per annum. Even allowing for a 10% fall off for circumstances beyond our advisers control this means a comfortable income but to do this entailed a lot of hard work, a great deal of running around and plenty of paperwork – in short, a huge effort.

Now, we will look at what happens when our adviser concentrates on their top twenty clients. Naturally, the average case size is bigger, it is now £1,200. Our adviser makes the list of their top twenty and has sixty gaps staring out from their referrals column. Our adviser calls each client in turn and explains that the individual is one of his most valued clients, in fact in his top twenty, and that from now on he will be delivering an even higher level of service than previously. Our adviser goes on to explain that because of the increased level of service for the client it will leave less time for marketing and this is where the client can help. "Mr client, I would appreciate your help, could you recommend just three individuals who may be suitable as clients for me. Obviously, you are unlikely to know their financial situation but you probably know three people just like you who fit my top twenty client profile: They care about their families and their business, they can make decisions and they have great economic potential." As before, you may want to make up your own criteria such as business owners or within a certain geographic area. The great thing about this approach is it gets easier as time goes by because very soon the people you are asking for referrals were originally referrals themselves, so it is a natural progression.

What if your worst nightmare came true? What if one of your top twenty clients you approached was horrified by your request and on the spot refused to ever do business with you again. Heck, this is even worse, lets just imagine three are so appalled by your request that they will never use you again. Don't panic! Of the remaining seventeen, eight give us the three referrals requested. Another eight can only think of one name and one client is delighted at being able to help and gives five referrals. We now have thirty-seven excellent prospects.

We'll assume our closing ratio does not change (it will go up, these are excellent prospects). We'll also assume that our average case size does not go up (it will go up, these are excellent prospects). If we convert 75% (27) at £1,200 it equates to production of £32,400. Even though this is a great idea I am not so naïve as to think it doesn't take time to convert prospects to clients so let's assume we carry out this exercise every other month, not every month (we wouldn't want to grow our businesses too fast, would we?! This equates to £194,400 of annual production. As these are excellent prospects we'll allow for just 5% fall-off of business for circumstances beyond our control. This means £185,000 of production. The very definition of working smarter, not harder! Remember, your top twenty clients are ever changing. The new names go on to the bottom for your next marketing push. The quality of your client base can only go up!

So far, the clients have an improved level of service and we have an expanding business and we are working a lot smarter. Now we need to remember those magic words, 'Thank You'! We described earlier how to calculate the cost of obtaining a client. This means we can build into our business a well-structured marketing budget so that we can 'speculate to accumulate'!

Here are seven referral ideas to take away and implement in your own practice. As well as showing how to say thank you to your top clients for their referrals I'm going to explain how to break into the corporate market, obtain your business suits at a discount and guarantee to make your spouse smile each week.

1. Take Clients on 'Appreciation Days'

These could be to sports events, the theatre, restaurants... I even took people up in a trip in a hot air balloon – the sky is the limit! I arranged a golf day especially for my clients in the medical profession. Each client that was invited brought along a colleague. We had the course professional give a group golf lesson and he then accompanied us around the course dispensing golf tips. Back at the famous '19th hole' a comedian entertained us for the evening. A good day out was had by all and a very large number of the guests became clients.

2. Give Gifts

We have spoken about business books but what about flowers or even holidays. After one client of mine had referred eight clients to me I presented him and his wife with a weekend stay in New York. Total production from the eight referrals was £34,500. My profit was £6,210. Cost of the holiday £3,300. How did the client feel? How did his wife feel!! How did I feel? Profit to me £2,910. Referrals since from the client have generated a further £5,400. Benefit to me in client goodwill – incalculable. If we really know our client we will probably know their hobbies and interests. What about sending a subscription to a specialist magazine. It has minimal cost and they will think of us 12 times a year.

3. Loyalty Cards

We have all seen the loyalty cards given by retailers and manufacturers. Why shouldn't we, as financial advisers, have one? My top twenty clients know they are part of an exclusive club. They are rewarded with points when a referral becomes a client. They can then swap these points for thank you gifts whenever they choose. These gifts range from tailored suits to fine wines, from days out, to computer equipment. You know what I have done behind the scenes? I explained to the service providers what I was doing and suggested that as I would be making repeat purchases over the year, I would like to arrange a volume discount. This is intriguing and begs people to ask what I do. "Well, funny you should ask ...!" If you want to break into the corporate market, I've just explained how. As a result of buying gifts for personal clients I now have corporate clients including a firm of tailors, a flight bookers, a corporate travel consultancy, a bookstore and a computer supplier amongst others. All of them are happy to provide me with their services at a discount, for example new suits and my laptop computer. I have also undertaken joint mailings with them containing special offers for each of our top clients and in most cases the value of the gifts are tax deductible. How do I make sure my wife is happy? Instead of obtaining a discount from the florist who supplies my client flowers, they send a bouquet of fresh flowers to my wife each week!

4. The 'Three Letter Approach' – not three pieces of mail, just A. S. K.
Explain to clients that all the time we spend prospecting is time spent away from their affairs. We then say "Please could you help me by suggesting the names of three people I could speak to. They should be trustworthy, entrepreneurial and able to make decisions – just like you". Often, the major objection in someone's mind before giving names is the worry that the people being referred will be angry or concerned that their details have been given out without their prior knowledge or consent. So, I always add a second statement "However, there is one rule I have which I will not break or bend for anyone – even you! There is no way I will contact any of these people until you have spoken to them first. Is that OK with you?"

5. The 'Marketing Push' – produces up to two hundred warm prospects in two days. (See Appendix A-7)
This seems too simple to be true but I've done it and it works. Call twenty clients on Monday. Explain we are on a marketing drive for new clients and ask if they could fax or email us a list of ten names and numbers by Wednesday. Make sure you use selection criteria as in the first ASK method. Say we have allocated Thursday and Friday to call these people and book appointments. Ask if the clients could call the people before Wednesday to let them know we will be calling. (Deadlines are important, people naturally want to meet them. This will fail if the request is open-ended.)

6. The 'Fact Find Finale' – With this the client will remind us to remind them to give 4 referrals
At the beginning of the meeting we place an envelope on the table with 'Thank You' written on it and ask the client not to let us forget it. At the end of the meeting they will remind us. We open it and take out a piece of paper, a large denomination banknote and an equivalent value gift voucher for an upmarket store. On the paper is space for four referrals including a telephone number and notes section. At the bottom is a space

for 'favourite charity'. We then explain that by the client completing the paper we make a donation (equivalent value to the banknote) to charity. If one referral becomes a client, we send the gift voucher to our original client and if both become clients we also send the banknote. Every referral received thereafter from the original client means they receive another cash sum and so does their charity.

7. The 'Post Sale Paragraph' – referrals by mail

In the UK it is compulsory after every sale to send a letter explaining the rationale behind the sale. If this is not compulsory in your state or country I urge you to consider it. It is highly likely to be mandatory one day and is good working practice. However, rather than view this as a chore, I view it as a way to obtain more referrals.

In our post sale letter, we have a 'P.S.' paragraph that says "Please remember that we do all our business by personal recommendation and referral. It helps us tremendously to go on providing our clients with the high level of service they expect and deserve if they assist us by giving us the details of anyone they feel we may be able to help. Your assistance in this would be most appreciated."

Note: Before implementing any of the concepts I've just described check with your state or country's insurance, tax or legal regulations pertaining to the giving of gifts to clients

How do the referral concepts appear? From the top twenty clients' perspective they are receiving excellent service, they have a relationship with a trusted adviser and they feel respected and appreciated. From our point of view, we are giving extraordinary value, we are being rewarded appropriately and our business is growing as we work smarter.

You can use the opportunity grid idea from Chapter 3 to list your top twenty clients and the referral ideas and work your way through until it is all coloured red.

In summary, it takes between three to nine months to move our practice from the old method of time consuming and expensive prospecting to a self-generating high-quality referral-based business.

In order to do this, we must:

1. Earn client trust;
2. Provide extraordinary service to our top twenty clients
3. Use goal setting for referrals;
4. Implement a marketing strategy; and
5. Always say 'Thank You' and remember to 'ASK'!

6.6 Blue - Prospecting without Referrals

For those that don't have sufficient QUALITY clients to obtain referrals from, I have summarised in brief a few other methods of prospecting that have been proven to work and a few that do not. If there had to be one phrase to summarise the secret of successful prospecting it would be 'meeting people under favourable circumstances'.

1. Define target market

Stage one is to define your target market. Who exactly do you want as clients and therefore who should you be prospecting? The old phrase "If you want to know what John Smith buys then you must look through John Smiths eyes" is very true. What do your target market want? Where do your target market live and work? What do they read?

What are their concerns and worries? When we know the answer to these questions and more, only then can we start to address them.

For example, if you want to target doctors, then become familiar with what doctors need by way of financial planning. What benefits do they get, when is the best time to call on them, what age do they retire and so on.

If we wish to target business owners, we should join our local chamber of commerce or start to work on joint ventures with accountancy firms. In short, do what business owners do, go where business owners go and talk like business owners talk.

Once your target market is defined and you know the kind of challenges they face and therefore the solutions that you can offer, we need to decide how we are going to contact these people.

A series of questions need to be considered:

- will it be by picking up the telephone?
- are we going to do it or will we pay a telesales professional?
- will the call follow up a mailing or will we use the post alone?
- how many calls do you need to make?
- what is the cost and success rate percentage of a direct mailing?

Not only should you find out these things before progressing, but it is also important to monitor your results. Only then will you know if your campaign is working or not. As with recruitment if you are to undertake prospecting by marketing methods other than referrals I urge you to employ a marketing professional. If done properly it will be instantly profitable although it will need a little initial capital. If this is beyond your means, then attend a seminar or read books on your chosen area of marketing such as direct mail.

2. What NOT to do

Be wary of printed adverts or having a space at exhibitions. These are notoriously difficult to prove profitable for the majority of financial advisers. For proof look at the adverts in the major financial newspapers. They are mostly direct offers or inferior products, both of which as face to face advisers we shouldn't be too interested in. We should not look to compete with the major direct offer giants as for the majority they will have deeper pockets than us and so win in a price cutting war. We get caught up in what is called 'commoditisation of products', simply trying to shift more and more of our wares (volume) and at a cheaper price (discount). I suggest leaving that to the companies with 'direct' in their name whilst we focus on quality. In addition, the regulatory requirement for 'small print' also has an effect. Advertising space that YOU are paying for is being used by the regulatory body for THEIR announcement. This is done in the name of consumer protection, yet I can't help but wonder how household name companies are allowed to get away with selling 10 or 20-year endowments. You know the ones, with a free alarm clock, travel bag or store vouchers, directly through mailers in tabloid newspapers! If an adviser recommended those high charged and inflexible products typically taken up by those on lower incomes, the adviser would be unlikely to see the case go through compliance. Yet they are allowed to survive. Perhaps a conspiracy theory for another day!

Financial exhibitions are notoriously attended by eternal 'browsers' in search of a free lunch. The expense and time involved rarely justify the results.

I am aware that in both printed advertisements and exhibition stands there will be success stories. Advertisement space sellers and exhibition organisers will disagree with me, but I maintain that the success stories are the exception rather than the rule.

3. Seminars

The most effective way to prospect outside of obtaining client referrals is seminar selling. (see Appendix A-3). Just like any other kind of prospecting, define your target market first. For example, do you want retirees with lump sums to invest or business owners? Your chosen market will then determine the seminar content. As with all aspects of our business, keep comprehensive data, running from the number of people invited, to who turns up on the day. Then log the number of appointments made and business completed thereafter. Remember to track the financials, how much does the seminar cost and what is the return? Keep the data as each seminar passes and start to calculate averages to avoid any 'data spikes' caused by one big investment or a coachload of attendees turning up! Don't just do one seminar. It needs to be a whole programme, running over the course of a year. The content can remain the same, with maybe topical items changed to keep it fresh but the fact is that the date you set will not be convenient for everyone. By running the seminar regularly those who could not attend on the first date will probably attend the second or third. And those who attend may recommend future dates to friends and colleagues. For the same reason aim to run more than one a day, perhaps having a morning session, a matinee and an evening.

Remember your first ever sales presentation to a prospect. Looking back, it probably wasn't that great! But as you have repeated it and become more confident over the years you could probably do it with your eyes shut now. It is the same with seminars. Don't expect miracles from day one but do persevere. Before starting, decide the number of seminars per day and the number over the year and budget accordingly in your business plan.

What now follows are a few tips to make your seminars a success:

- start 5 minutes late so that interruptions by latecomers are minimised;
- avoid dates that clash with major events (royal weddings, sports finals, public holidays);
- your chosen venue should have
  sufficient parking
  professional staff and
  should be within 20 minutes travel time for attendees
- you should aim for 25 attendees;
- ensure that your chosen room can be 'shrunk' or 'enlarged' in case the numbers that turn up are wildly different from those expected;
- choose an air-conditioned venue;
- do not serve alcohol;
- dress to impress; and
- guide attendees in to fill up chairs from the front

Experience has shown that it is not the day itself that is the hard part but more likely the initial act of 'getting bums on seats'. I know of advisers who run excellent seminars who have trained and operate their own direct mailing and telesales follow up operation. By keeping it all in house, they retain control and have lower costs.

At my company we decided to outsource this and engaged a telesales company to oversee the whole operation. Although this increased the cost we were given a guarantee of the number of attendees and also a 'quality threshold', meaning that if anyone who arrived was only there for the free sandwiches they would replace the name free of charge.

Generally, the aim of the seminar should be as a call to action and leave the attendees wanting a face to face meeting. The seminar should serve a dual purpose, firstly informing the attendees that they have a problem and secondly, letting them know that we are the ones to solve it.

4. Networking and professional introducers

By networking I do not mean the rightly maligned pyramid type organisations but rather simply increasing the number of mutually beneficial win-win relationships that you have with other people or organisations. At a simple level and on a one-to-one basis the most popular form is that of professional introducers. Typically, a good introducer of business to a financial adviser is an accountant or a solicitor. Increasingly, as specialisation becomes the norm, there may be a need for different relationships with the two practices, for example the conveyancing partner at the solicitor partnering with a mortgage expert and the corporate lawyer linking with a business insurance specialist.

Although these two are often the first to spring to mind, with a little thought the others come thick and fast. There are other obvious examples such as estate agents, general insurance brokers or management consultants. These will all have the need to outsource certain tasks to financial services professionals.

With networking the situation must not be one sided and to be successful it must be win-win. At a basic level the financial adviser could simply make a cash payment to the introducer as a thank you for the introduced business, but this can cause ethical problems in some professions. A more mutually acceptable outcome may be to send clients back the other way, for example recommending the conveyancing solicitor to your mortgage clients and the accountant to those who need to complete a tax return.

There are many organisations who realise that the above arrangements can really work and have set up formal alliances to assist those who wish to refer. These often take the form of breakfast meetings or business lunches.

Whilst setting up your own select group of professional introducers is often the most attractive route to go, everyone involved must be aware of the parameters in which you will be working. Are payments to be made, if so, how much? How should referrals be treated, what is to happen if the relationship becomes one sided and so on.

The professional networking organisations will have all the answers to these questions but be wary of those that charge a high fixed fee and insist on a certain number of referrals being given every meeting as this can often lead to bad feelings and substandard referrals being given simply to hit quotas.

If networking ethically is a method you wish to try then my advice is to start with your local chamber of commerce. The meetings and networking events will be with other business people (for that is what we are) all looking to improve and further their business. If you approach with a long-term view of helping others then you will succeed. You must be genuinely interested in those that you speak with. A good opening question is "How did you get started in your business?" Be prepared for the floodgates to open. We all love to talk about our business and ourselves and in a room full of people wanting to tell their story someone who will listen is a valuable commodity!

If you approach networking by viewing a room of strangers who could do business immediately to be ticked or crossed off a list then you are doomed to failure. You must build an excellent reputation, mostly by being honest, trustworthy and knowledgeable and then the introductions will flow.

5. Newsletters

In Chapter 6.5, on referrals, I showed that to obtain quality referrals there may be a better use of your resources than sending a client newsletter, the thinking being that by sending a newsletter to all clients, you may get referrals from all clients and the aim should be to take referrals from the best only. That aside, a newsletter can be an excellent way to keep your name in front of people. Writing a newsletter is an art and is probably best left to those who do it for a living. As a professional financial adviser and amateur author myself, I can vouch for how long it takes to ensure a publication or article has no errors or omissions and it seems that no matter how many times an article is checked, there is often a small typographical error left on publication! Once you add in all the compliance problems this could create then you can see the sense in outsourcing this work. There are a number of companies who will provide a monthly or quarterly newsletter for you. They create all the content and make sure it is compliant and your details are overprinted on the cover giving the impression it is yours alone. These can range from a few pence for a single sheet black and white page to a few pounds for a full colour multi-page magazine. Remember to include the cost of envelopes and postage when entering your newsletter budget into your business plan.

A popular spin off today is the electronic newsletter. This has the advantage of being considerably cheaper than the traditional paper version but naturally has less inherent perceived value in the eyes of the recipient as many clients are aware of the transient nature of electronic information. If you are going to produce an e-newsletter make sure that it uses technology by being personalised and eye-catching. One other benefit of electronic newsletters are that they are relatively inexpensive and easy to store as a resource on your website. Clients can in turn search through them, saving you money and enabling clients to obtain information at a time convenient to them, not just when you are available.

CHAPTER 7

THE DAILY POINTS SYSTEM

So to recap on the colours:

- Red – face-to-face;
- Blue – prospecting;
- Green – personal;
- Yellow – travel; and
- Black – administration.

At the end of each day, we should spend 5 minutes totalling how long, as a percentage of our day, we spent in each of the colours. On a Friday spend 10 minutes totalling the week and at the end of every 4 weeks spend 30 minutes reviewing the 'month' – Remember we have 13 'months' of 4 weeks in the year.

By using just a few of the Success Plan concepts most of us should be able to gain an extra 4 weeks by having 13 'months' instead of 12, an extra 8 hours by restructuring or not travelling and an extra 10-20 hours by delegating.

Consider what we would call a perfect week. Mine is Diagram 7.1. We should plan it in our diary putting in spaces for client meetings, time with our family, catching up on admin and so on. Stick to it. Don't let clients dictate when we see them. Ask them what appointment slot they would like and give a choice. Remember this is your Success Plan. You are in charge and you define success. We may want appointments spread out across the week or to concentrate them in a few days. Our industry is littered with different styles and approaches. Find out what works for you. For everyone who dreams of writing £1,000,000 and working 8 days a week to achieve it there is someone who wants to spend little time at work and as much time as possible with their family and there are those who'd like both!

In the example the grey time is spare. We can attend to business management issues, take part in training sessions, attend to personal matters, in fact the grey can end up as any colour at all. When doing our own planner we may end up with more grey than the example or none at all. What is important is that we have planned all the other time in advance.

Diagram 7.1 – Ideal Week

Have a look at Diagram 7.2. This is the daily target system that lies at the heart of the Success Plan. It provides an ongoing record of our activity and satisfactory completion guarantees success. It also has a fail-safe mechanism so that if things are going wrong we can immediately see the area that needs improving or changing. On the flip side, we will also be able to spot areas that are working and build on those strengths.

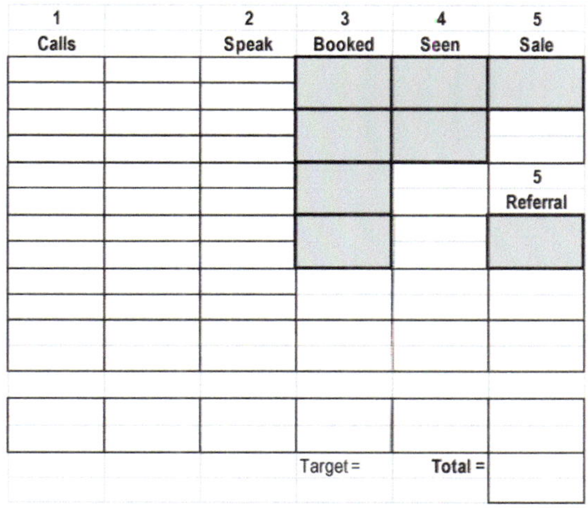

1 point = make a call

2 points = meaningful conversation

3 points = book an appointment

4 points = kept appointment

5 points = sale / fee earned

5 points = each referral

Diagram 7.2 – The Daily Points System

So how does it work? Each day, to be successful in our practices and achieve our goals there are a number of things we need to do.

At my first MDRT meeting I heard this phrase "Success or greatness is a matter of small numbers, one more telephone call, one more appointment, one more time through the proposal ...". (See Appendix A-8.)

This is basic stuff and we are all taught it from day one in the industry, just as I was as mentioned in Chapter 2 but I'm just going to confirm and print it again now.

It's called 'the Sales Circle'.

Going over this reminds me of the line "Did you ever have a sales idea so good, you stopped using it?" That is what this is. It is so simple and we all used to do it but then we became successful and stopped!

Every piece of business starts with picking up the 'phone. It may be a cold call, a referral, an advertising lead or something else but we have to pick up the 'phone. Then we have to speak with the prospect and book a meeting. We have to actually carry out the meeting and make a sale. Lastly we need to ask for a referral so that we can start the Sales circle again.

This is simple stuff, the building blocks of our profession, but we still have to do them, from the new recruit on day one to the twenty-five year experienced adviser. If we don't do each stage of the sales circle and keep going round and round then our income dries up.

Each stage of the Sales Circle goes onto the grid and each stage has a points value. The harder the task, the more points we score for completing it. To guarantee success we need to score a set number of points each day.

Points are awarded as follows:

1 point – each time we dial a number on the telephone, whether we get to speak to someone or not;
2 points – each time we speak to a client or prospect;
3 points – each time we book a meeting;
4 points – each time we hold a meeting with a client or prospect;
5 points – each time we make a sale or obtain a referral.

The Success Plan magic number is seventy-four. In other words, to guarantee success we need seventy-four points each day.

If we want to guarantee success, we need seventy-four points per day.

I don't know why, it just is! I've tried fifty and it isn't enough and I've tried one hundred and it's too many. I suggest it is made up as follows:

5 points for each sale;
5 points for each referral;
12 points for three meetings;
12 points for four meetings booked;
20 points for speaking to ten people;
20 points for twenty telephone calls.

There are, of course, many, many combinations of making the seventy-four points. However, we do it, seventy-four works.

It all starts at the beginning of the Sales Circle. If we have absolutely no prospects we are going to have to pick up the yellow pages or buy a calling list and start calling. We may need to make fifty calls to get our seventy-four points, but then we are off and running. As we get better on the telephone we won't need to make so many calls to speak to the people and the points add up quicker. Once we are talking to the right people it is easier to make appointments.

As we carry out an action, tick a box to record it. There is extra room at the bottom of each column to record an action if we go over target.

If we are saying the right things to the right people then most of our meetings should be taking place. I'll assume that most readers will know what to say when in front of prospects (if not, seek out advice from those advisers and agents in your company you respect or attend an LIA or MDRT meeting and ask anyone you meet) and this translates into sales and higher points. From a sale a prospect becomes a client who should have no objection to giving us referrals, so starting over again.

Most of my business comes from client or professional connection referrals so I build up points that way. But the circle won't keep going unless I 'phone them, speak to them and give a compelling reason to meet, see them and show I can create value in their lives and ultimately complete some business. Every time I still have to obtain more referrals.

The suggested combination above should take no more than 5.5 hours per day:

30 minutes calling;
1 hour speaking to the ten people;
4 hours seeing two people;
Leaving the rest of the day for personal time, admin, etc.

By combining the points system with the diary planner and time analysis we have everything we need to guarantee success every day of the week on one sheet of paper. We should keep this sheet in front of us on our desks as a constant reminder of our daily goals.

There is a blank example on Diagram 7.3 and a completed example on Diagram 7.4. See how the points are added up at the bottom of the columns reflecting the days activity. The segments are coloured in alongside the appointments and tasks at the bottom of each day are the total time spent in each colour activity.

Diagram 7.3 – The Success Planner Blank

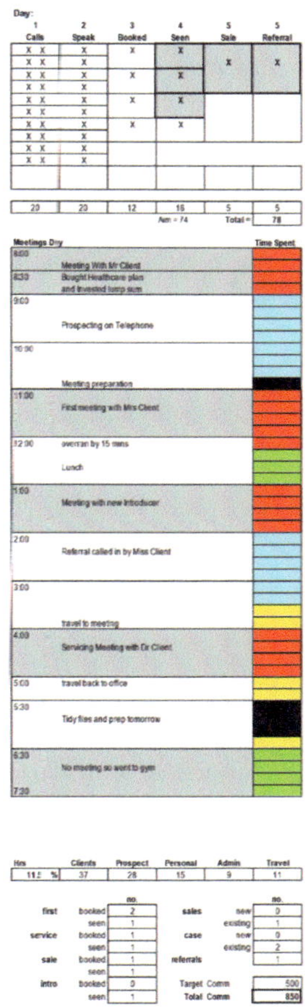

Diagram 7.4 – The Success Planner Completed

We should keep a stock of these blank planners in front of us, with the dates above each day. I always have a rolling twelve-week set, enabling me to plan my diary three months ahead. To make it easier to use we have it blown up on a copier to desk jotter size.

There is also a powerful set of goal planners and analysis tools that go with the one page Success Plan enabling us to track our vital business statistics, such as our number of first meetings, closing ratios, progress on yearly production targets, ongoing average case size and hourly rate, amongst others.

Over the years there have been a number of successful business tracking and analysis systems and all have their pros and cons. Some use less data than the Success Plan, others use more. More data can lead to deeper insight, but there is also the danger of information overload leading to deeper confusion! Too little data helps no one.

I suggest that for new entrants to financial services keeping the record of meetings held, meetings cancelled and product and sales, to meetings ratios is good business practice. It will help you to spot any challenges you may face sooner rather than later. For example, if you are booking meetings and people are turning up but the sales don't seem to be following you can look to technical training or sales skills. You will probably also find that referrals are not forthcoming either. One of the other truths of the Sales Circle is that you have to go right the way round, in the right order and stopping at every stage to be able to complete the circle. There are no short cuts. At the outset of a career it is important to know your ratios. The famous 'one-card' system (see Appendix A-9) used in many agencies in the USA presumes ten calls leads to three appointments leading to one sale. So to make four sales basic mathematics says we need to make forty calls.

Once, I was comfortable and confident on the telephone as well as practised in my presentations I found I had an overall two out of three (or 66%) success rate. I'd book three meetings of which two would turn up. In addition of every three that turned up, two would become clients. Build in my call ratio of five calls for two appointments and I knew I had to make twenty-three calls to make four sales.

In those days picking up the phone, at the start of the Sales Circle, needed to be done twenty-three times to hit the target. Now it is more like four or five calls to make four sales but without all that practising I wouldn't have been able to get to today's ratios. And without keeping track I wouldn't have known if I was improving or deteriorating. To see my ratios coming down was one of the key factors that kept me going in the early days. It proved to me that I was getting better and as I saw my successful sales ratio improving too I knew that I was good at my job.

For more experienced advisers it is likely that the number of clients not turning up for meetings, or the number of 'closing meetings' where a sale is not made are very small. That is not to undermine the data but you may feel that you are at a stage where so few meetings don't happen for genuine reasons that the figures are not worth tracking. The same principle also applies with calls. The experienced adviser will probably reach a stage where nearly all calls result in a meeting, again rendering the tracking and analysis of such data unnecessary. Why do more work than you have to?

The section at the base of each day on the Success Planner is where you log your activity and production (look back to Diagrams 7.3 and 7.4). For the experienced adviser this will usually take the form of a number of meetings, split into first, servicing, then sales and introducers. Sales are logged and broken into the number of cases and whether from new or existing clients. Each number of referrals received are also recorded as is actual production for the day against daily target production.

In addition, the new adviser should record the number of meetings booked, split as above, into first, servicing, then sales and introducers. This will help the new adviser to monitor how their calling is going and what their turn-up rates are like. If a new adviser has a lot of meetings but all with existing clients or people they already know, there is a likelihood of a slow-down around the corner as the sales potential on these people will soon run out. The adviser needs to book in more new people, either by cold calling, marketing or the preferred method of obtaining referrals.

These figures are then totaled weekly, along with the hours spent in each of the colour sections (red – face-to-face; blue – prospecting; green – personal; yellow – travel; or black – admin.) and every four weeks (our 'month') the figures are transferred to the activity spreadsheet.

Pd	Days			Calls	Booked					Seen					Cases	Refs	Prod			Hrs	%					£/hr
	Sales	Admin	Off		First	Serv	Sale	Intro	Total	First	Serv	Sale	Intro	Total			New	Existing	Total		Clients	Prosp	Pers	Admin	Travel	
1	12	9	7	80	21	16	21	6	64	14	12	18	4	48	21	15	4600	5900	10500	220	40	20	10	20	10	48
2	14	8	6	93	18	12	20	4	54	13	10	13	3	39	18	12	5800	5200	11000	180	45	15	10	20	10	61
3	10	10	8	102	24	28	22	4	78	18	20	16	4	58	20	10	6800	8200	15000	190	55	10	5	15	15	79
4	13	9	6	50	14	12	16	2	44	12	12	16	2	42	26	8	21000	9000	30000	210	70	10	5	5	10	143
5	6	8	14	32	10	5	5	1	21	8	5	5	1	19	8	2	1000	4000	5000	96	35	10	40	10	5	52
6	...	...	...	...	...	...	...	...	...	...	...	...	...	...	...	...	...	...	...	...	...	...	...	...	...	...
7																										
⋮																										
13																										
Total	...	...	...	...	...	...	...	...	...	...	...	...	...	...	...	...	...	...	...	...	...	...	...	...	...	...

Pd	Cases				Gross Production				Target GB	Variance	Issued		Target GB	Variance	Av Case
	new	exist	total	ytd	new	exist	total	ytd	gross		pm	ytd	net		
1	9	12	21	21	4600	5900	10500	10500	8,500	2000	8,000	8000	7,700	300	500
2	10	8	18	39	6000	5000	11000	21500	17,000	4500	7,500	15500	15,400	100	611
3	11	9	20	59	9000	6000	15000	36500	25,500	11000	22,500	38000	23,100	14,900	750
4	18	8	26	85	18000	12000	30000	66500	34,000	32500	5,500	43500	30,800	12,700	1154
5	3	5	8	93	1500	3500	5000	71500	42,500	29000	12,000	55500	38,500	17,000	625
6									51,000				46,200		
7									59,500				53,900		
8									68,000				61,600		
9									76,500				69,300		
10									85,000				77,000		
11									93,500				84,700		
12									102,000				92,400		
13									110,500				100,100		

Diagram 7.5 – Activity

As you can see from the partial year in the top grid of Diagram 7.5 the figures I track on activity are just as above, namely the number of sales days, number of admin days and number of days off. These always total twenty-eight as I work in four-week blocks. Meetings seen are taken directly from the main page of the planner and broken down into firsts, servicing, closing and introducers.

New advisers may also wish to do the same with calls so that they can monitor calls to turn up ratios. The number of cases (or applications) are next to the number of referrals. Total production is also broken down into production from new or existing clients. The total amount of hours spent at work is broken down into face-to-face time, prospecting (seminars), personal time, travel time and admin (remember the colours). Finally, the £ per hour rate is calculated. This is a key figure. If we have no idea of our true worth, how can we charge clients a realistic rate or even hope to make a profit? To refresh your memory on calculating your hourly target rate to measure against this actual, re-read Chapter 5.

The production figures from the main page of the Success Plan are then transferred onto a second spreadsheet (the lower grid of Diagram 7.5). Written and issued figures are then plotted on a graph (see Diagram 7.6) against targets to give an instant snapshot of progress for the year to date. Notice how the targets for written and issued are slightly different to allow for fall-off of business due to circumstances beyond our control. These figures are then analysed to provide an ongoing average case size. Average case size is also important to measure progress although some advisers like to gauge whether they should take on a new client not by single case size but by total average earnings in a year. I actually do both as I think the average income from a client in a year tells us whether we can afford to be working with them but the average case size has great importance when planning our Work In Progress (WIP) lists (see Chapter 9).

Finally, these monthly (a 'month' is a four week period – remember as that way there are thirteen of them) figures are inserted into a 'Top 20' (Diagram 7.7) showing best ever performance to guard against apathy and contentment and ensure constant forward movement. Just as it is for pop stars, it is great to see a recent month 'go straight in at number one' and if your top ten best months are all from a few years back then it is unlikely that your business is growing and profits are increasing.

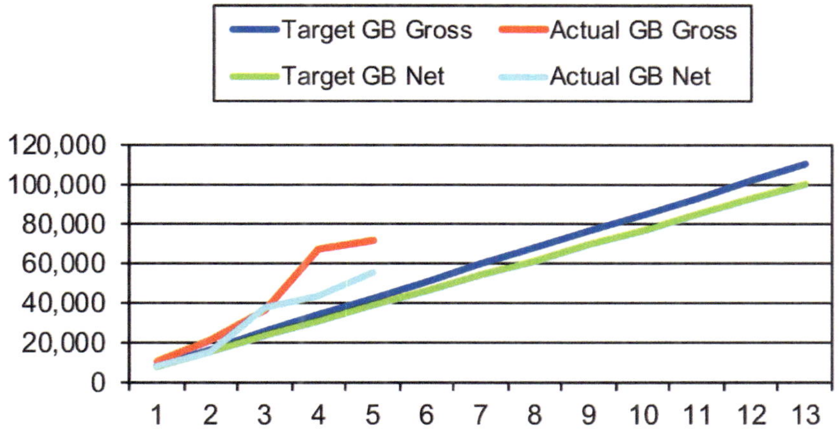

Diagram 7.6 – Year to Date

Month	Written	Cases	Average
Dec-00	56,480	33	1712
Aug-01	40,735	22	1852
Aug-00	33,459	25	1338
Mar-98	31,778	32	993
Mar-99	23,859	22	1085
Mar-00	23,693	21	1128
Jun-01	21,308	18	1184
Feb-00	19,746	14	1410
May-98	19,438	19	1023
May-01	18,482	17	1087
Apr-00	17,035	11	1549
Feb-99	15,214	16	951
Nov-98	14,325	19	754
Feb-98	14,317	15	954
Sep-00	14,131	10	1413
Mar-97	14,125	33	428
Nov-99	13,034	20	652
Apr-99	12,714	9	1413
Jun-98	11,829	6	1972
Sep-98	11,537	15	769

Diagram 7.7 – Top Twenty Months

I also like to keep a business ledger. In years gone by this was an old red book but it is now kept on computer and as a nod to the past the filename is 'redbook.xls'! The business ledger (Diagram 7.8) keeps track of all the data needed for my personal records but has the dual

Date	Client	Cons	Company	Product	Premium	M/A/S	Gross GB	Prop Date	Submitted		Status	Pol No.
27-Jun-00	F Bloggs	IG	Scot Eq	PMI	9.21	M	191.77	8-Jun-00	1-Jul-00		In force	123d
30-Jun-00	N Normal	AC	Standard Life	PP	83.33	M	715.78	8-Jun-00	3-Jul-00		In force	abd4
30-Jun-00	N Normal	IG	Fidelity	ISA	65.00	M	0.00	8-Jun-00	3-Jul-00	907.55	In force	x45t
3-Jul-00	K Smith	IG	Fidelity	ISA	7000.00	A	210.00	29-Jun-00	5-Jul-00		In force	5th7
3-Jul-00	M Roddell	AC	Fidelity	ISA	350.00	M	10.50	29-Jun-00	5-Jul-00		In force	hjk9
3-Jul-00	V Williams	HJ	Fidelity	ISA	1000.00	S	30.00	24-Jun-00	5-Jul-00		In force	00x2
6-Jul-00	V Williams	HJ	Fidelity	ISA	350.00	M	10.50	24-Jun-00	7-Jul-00		In force	123-876
9-Jul-00	R Camderwell	IG	Fidelity	ISA	5000.00	S	150.00	19-Jun-00	10-Jul-00		In force	345-gft
12-Jul-00	R Camderwell	IG	Norwich Union	Bond	20000.00	S	600.00	19-Jun-00	17-Jul-00		In force	345r
12-Jul-00	O Tipper	AC	Fidelity	U/T	68.00	M	2.00	27-Jun-00	17-Jul-00		In force	fgt432
15-Jul-00	O Tipper	IG	Norwich Union	PP	85.90	A	737.86	27-Jun-00	17-Jul-00		In force	456hdg
15-Jul-00	N Portman	MR	Standard Life	PP	192.31	M	1710.89	28-Jun-00	17-Jul-00		Lapsed	345sdf
17-Jul-00	S Bayliss	IG	Norwich Union	IHT	201.60	M	1731.69	13-Jul-00	17-Jul-00		Lapsed	345-yu
17-Jul-00	S Bayliss	IG	Norwich Union	IHT	887.50	S	49.70	13-Jul-00	17-Jul-00		In force	45fg
20-Jul-00	S Jones	IG	Norwich Union	PP	90.00	M	776.44	30-Jun-00	21-Jul-00		In force	45gh-uuy
21-Jul-00	A Samson	AC	Skandia	Bond	30000.00	S	900.76	19-Jul-00	21-Jul-00		In force	ewrt54
21-Jul-00	A Samson	AC	Skandia	U/T	500.00	M	15.00	19-Jul-00	21-Jul-00		In force	c876-0
21-Jul-00	D Glover	MR	Skandia	U/T	200.00	M	6.00	7-Jul-00	21-Jul-00	6941.34	In force	vsg344
2-Aug-00	C Appleyard	AC	Scot Widows	PP	189.10	M	1624.35	28-Jul-00	2-Aug-00		In force	4r554r
2-Aug-00	B Little	HJ	Framlington	ISA	7000.00	S	210.00	1-Aug-00	2-Aug-00		In force	4355gs
2-Aug-00	J Long	MR	Skandia	ISA	7000.00	S	210.00	1-Aug-00	2-Aug-00		In force	897g5
2-Aug-00	V Williams	AC	Norwich Union	ISA	7000.00	S	210.00	1-Aug-00	2-Aug-00		In force	879er
2-Aug-00	V Williams	AC	Axa Sun Life	Bond	33200.00	S	996.00	1-Aug-00	2-Aug-00		In force	132fg
2-Aug-00	V Williams	AC	Norwich Union	Bond	100000.00	S	3000.00	1-Aug-00	2-Aug-00		In force	3124ghj
3-Aug-00	R Bishop	IG	Scot Life	PMI	206.53	M	3216.62	13-Jun-00	3-Aug-00		In force	45bng
3-Aug-00	R Bishop	IG	Scot Life	PHI	41.99	M	615.18	14-Jun-00	4-Aug-00		In force	56ghj

Diagram 7.8 – The Red Book Sales Ledger

purpose of being able to provide those all important Key Performance Indicators (KPIs) needed for ongoing compliance and training and competency reviews.

The headings are:

- a unique case reference for use on correspondence;
- the date the paperwork was completed;
- the client name;
- the adviser
- the provider (not required if you only work for one company);
- the product;
- the premium and frequency;
- the commission or fees generated;
- the date the proposal was signed;
- the date submitted to the life company and the status of the policy;
- the policy number, when issued.

By using a standard format for each of the columns, searches and analysis can be carried out quickly and easily. For example, personal pensions are always entered as PP. All staff are aware of this as if different people entered things in different formats (e.g. P.P.P. or PersPen instead of PP) the analysis could not happen. By keeping the different dates you can also track how long a case takes to go through your admin processes, useful for identifying staff training needs, or how long life companies take to process paperwork. Useful when making client recommendations!

Because you can search and sort the data with ease it is a simple matter to tally up how much of your income is down to a particular product type or who your ten most profitable clients are. These facts and many more are invaluable for today's adviser who, due to economic forces, must be aware of issues such as profitability if they are to prosper in the modern '1% world' of reduced commissions.

There are complex and expensive computer programmes available that will do all the above for you. I started out with a sheet of grid paper and now use a simple spreadsheet programme popular on most PCs. All the analysis calculations were worked out using the 'help file' on the programme. It is not rocket science but a basic grasp of maths is needed although some would argue that is a pre-requisite for a financial adviser anyway!

By combining the daily statistics from the one page Success Plan and the monthly analysis sheets with the target figures worked out at the beginning of the book, we now have a complete action plan that we can use to guarantee success every single day. We know how many days we have to work and what we need to do and produce each day to hit our annual target. There are no excuses left for not hitting the target. There may be valid reasons, such as "I was ill", but there are no excuses. If you did not hit your target or reach your definition of success you will be able to see exactly why, from not making the calls through to not asking for referrals, from not seeing enough people to spending too much time doing admin. Importantly if we do identify the reasons for not hitting our targets we also have the tools within this book to learn from our experience. If we learn from an experience, it is not a failure. The only time we can fail is if we quit.

Our appointments or empty slots are in front of us. The analysis pages alert us to any peaks or troughs ahead and confirm our successes. The daily seventy-four points target forces consistency. This is often the big challenge for many of us.

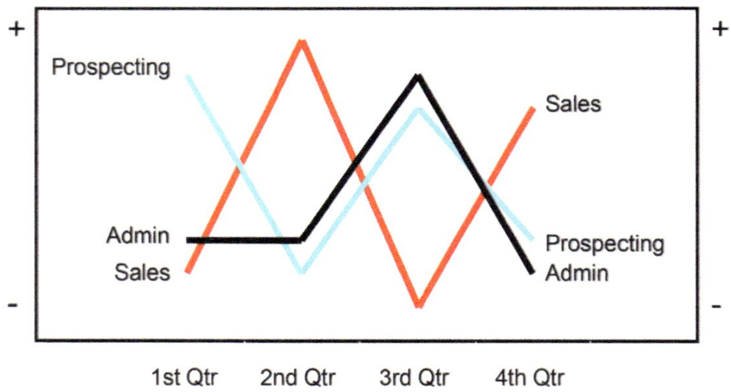

Diagram 7.9 – Task Graph

We have a period of prospecting that creates many sales and lots of money. But all those sales force us into lots of admin and before we know it we haven't prospected for a week and the diary is empty. Back on the 'phones to fill up the diary but now we are behind on the admin (see Diagram

7.9). As we discussed earlier it is simple to get caught up in the business, take our eye off the ball and find ourselves behind on sales, prospecting, admin or all of them!

If we are not being successful, by our standards, we will be able to see why and remedy it. The points system is not only an incredible goal setting tool to show us what we need to do to succeed but it is also an amazing analytical tool that can show us what we are doing right or where we are going wrong.

The points system keeps us focused every day on what we need to do and the moment we see a fall-off in points in one area we know where to take remedial action before it is too late. This was touched on briefly in an earlier section but to recap:

For example:

If we are making twenty calls but not speaking with ten people we may be calling the wrong people or at the wrong time, or both. It is no good calling Futures Traders when the markets are open, they are busy. Get them when the market is closed. It is easy to call secretaries, but we have to ask if they are the right target market.

If we are speaking to ten people but not booking four meetings, we are saying the wrong things, so consider going on a telephone course or have voice coaching. Come up with a line or two that will make prospects interested. There are sales ideas throughout this book. Just one, learnt and practiced will be enough. Match your area of expertise and the reason for the call to the prospect. For example, tell lawyers about estate planning and accountants about tax breaks, not vice versa.

If we are booking four but not seeing two:

- we are not confirming meetings or not giving a compelling enough reason for the prospect to turn up.

If we are seeing two but not selling one:

- we may need sales training, technical knowledge or need to tighten our closing.

If we are not obtaining referrals:

- we are probably not asking, or not providing sufficiently high standards in customer service.

The analysis can go further still. We may notice that we are great at making sales and obtaining referrals but it takes a lot of calling to get a meeting. We could then consider delegating the appointment meeting to a specialist. Once we start to use the Success Plan we will find other ways to adapt it to our way of working.

In summary, we should spend a whole day, with no interruptions, working out our own Success Plan layout.

Starting with:

- how much do we want to earn? (target); and
- how long do we want to take to earn it? (days at work and daily production required);
- then calculate our average case size and closing ratios to determine how many meetings we will need;
- goal set these meeting spaces in The Success Plan alongside personal and family time;
- inform clients of the new working practice remembering to explain the benefits to them;
- track your activity each day, every 15 minutes (or 6 for fee charging) and total at the end of each day and each week;
- ensure you reach 74 points every day.

Use the Success Plan concepts to improve your colours:

- **Red** – Face-to-Face with Clients
  See clients in your meeting slots
  Send out a pre-meeting fact-find questionnaire;

- **Blue** – Prospecting (Referrals)
  Implement the five referral concepts with your best clients
  Send the Opportunity Jigsaw to qualified corporate clients;

- **Yellow** – Travel
  Work in-house or in a local office environment
  Have a localised diary (Tuesdays = Downtown etc);

- **Green** – Personal or Family Time
  Book it in your diary and make it a priority;

- **Black** – Administration
  Delegate all £10 per hour work and focus on £260 per hour tasks.

You will need to work the Success Plan for at least four weeks to obtain the maximum benefit and prove to yourself it really works. That means you have to put in a little hard work but then no one said this job was easy.

After twelve weeks you will see an incredible difference and if my own experience is anything to go by in one year or less you should have doubled your income and be working at least 25% less hours.

It is an old phrase, but a good one. "Nobody plans to fail, they just fail to plan"

It worked for me and I know that if you commit to carrying it out and following through then The Success Plan will work for you, whatever your definition of success is.

SECTION 3

CHAPTER 8

FEE CHARGING

This is a subject that provokes controversy and conversation whenever it is raised. Commission has been the backbone of the life insurance and financial planning profession for a long time. There are those who say it should remain so and there are those who maintain that fee charging is the only way to remain in business. This chapter is not about trying to resolve that issue. This chapter will show you how fee charging, if you choose to adopt it in full or in part in your practice, needn't be a problem.

If you have followed the Success Plan so far then you should know your expenses for the year (covered in Chapter 4) and your personal production target as well as your hourly rate (covered in Chapter 5). If your expenses are £36,000 a year and target is £100,000 and you intend to work for 200 x 10 hour days your minimum rate to cover expenses is £18. To hit target and make a profit you could charge £50.

However, it is unlikely that you will be able to charge out all of your hours. Many legal practices like their fee earners to be billing 1200 hours per year, considerably less than the 2000 hours above. On a year consisting of 200 days at work that is 6 hours a day billable to clients. If we use this as a more realistic goal than charging 100% of our time the hourly rates increase dramatically. To cover expenses the rate is £30 and to hit target £84. On the basis that we don't want to work any harder than 200 x 10 hour days if your annual target is higher the only option is to increase fees, so for example a target of £200,000 will need an hourly rate of £168.

We must track our time carefully. We should take a leaf out of the books of our fellow professionals, the lawyers and accountants and have a daily time sheet.

To achieve this we simply split our diary into months, then weeks, then days, then hours, then six minute segments. Many of us may already have a diary set out like this, that is fine! If not, feel free to use the format in Diagram 8.1 below.

	Time	Client	Notes	6 minute segments	Chargable ?
8:00am					
9:00am					
10:00am					
11:00am					
12:00noon					
1:00pm					
2:00pm					
3:00pm					
4:00pm					
5:00pm					
6:00pm					
7:00pm+					

Diagram 8.1 – The Time Sheet

We can see the hours are broken down into six-minute segments. That doesn't mean we have to stop work every six minutes to fill it in, but six minutes is a good unit of time to complete a small task, and there are ten six minute segments every hour so the maths is easy when calculating a client bill!

The 'client' heading is self-explanatory but can be useful for other things too, such as differentiating between personal work and corporate work for the same person, such as a business owner.

The main section, headed 'notes', is of invaluable help when we come to invoice a client for work carried out as we have an ongoing log of all work completed in precise terms. In this ever more litigious society we live in, detailed records such as this could prove to be our greatest asset should disputes ever arise.

The last column should be ticked if the time we spend is chargeable to the client.

I suggest we keep the time sheet in front of us all day, updating it every time we finish a task, such as working on a client file or talking on the telephone.

The time sheet can easily be incorporated into the Success Planner by simply logging tasks completed into the main box and changing the fifteen-minute segments to six-minute segments and ticking next to the coloured boxes if the work is chargeable.

I am not suggesting that we bill every last second to the client or start the clock every time someone calls but by completing the time sheet we see clearly just how long we spend on a client's affairs. How we use that information is up to us, for example the decision on whether to charge a client for the time we spend on 'hold' to a life company is ours.

I truly believe that by completing the sheet we will start to value our time more highly and be aware of when we are spending time doing tasks better suited to a lower paid individual.

Another by-product is that as the days and weeks pass and we spend more of our time in the £260 per hour zone (in Success Planner terms, the red pen) rather than the £10 per hour zone (the black pen) the sheets act as a good way to prove to ourselves that more staff are needed. It will demonstrate that by employing another person, and delegating wisely, our turnover and profits will increase.

For some advisers the move to charging fees can be seen as a negative. But as with everything, change can bring opportunity and therefore fees should be viewed as positive. How do we do this? Why not use fees to obtain more referrals? When presenting your final invoice, leave room at the bottom for a discount. Each referral given qualifies the client for a discount of, say £100, from the invoice. Make sure you still apply all the referral rules listed in Chapter 6.5 such as prequalification with a quality threshold but it is another win-win-win scenario. What client wouldn't want to help you maximise time on their affairs by minimising your marketing efforts, especially if it saves them money on their bill? They save money, we get more quality referrals and a new client has the benefit of our excellent services. Naturally the discount only becomes effective when the referred names become clients and the original client has the option of a refund by way of cheque or the discount applied to their next bill.

I believe that by gaining more of an insight into our true hourly worth we will become more profitable and ultimately be able to provide a better service to our clients.

CHAPTER 9

THREE 'MUST HAVE' BUSINESS MANAGEMENT TOOLS:

WIP List, Agenda, Trackers

W.I.P. list

Have a WIP List (Work In Progress) (see Diagram 9.1 overleaf). This was mentioned in chapter 7 and is your early warning system. It should list every single piece of potential work you know of. My WIP list has a column headed 'Called', to note when I called the prospect/client and a column to show when they are booked in. Even these first two simple columns eradicate a simple query for many advisers, who should I call? If there is a piece of business and a blank space in the 'called column' you have your call list for the day (remember the first stage of the sales circle? Pick up the 'phone). The client is then named along with the products they are interested in and a notes section.

The next three columns are the key to 'Forward Planning'. If you are absolutely certain the business will transact in the current four-week period then put the amount of fees or commission expected in the 'Definite' column. It should always be the case that unless a client is booked in, the amount cannot possibly be definite. If it is not in the diary, the sale cannot be made. Some advisers would say that a possible exception to this rule is if the business is in the post. I have been let down by the postal system and clients being economical with the truth too many times to allow this, so any business 'in the post' remains in the next column, that of maybe!

Any work that you foresee completing in the next six/eight weeks should go here. Business planned for more than eight weeks into the future should go on a second page of the WIP list as, although planned, it is too far away to be certain and unlikely to impact on cash flow. It can be dropped into the first page when appropriate. The final column is completed business, and amounts should be entered in here only when the case is submitted.

We should really take out our WIP list in the first week of the month

ian-stats

		Work In Progress (WIP) List					June
Called	Booked	Name	Definite	Maybe	Complete	Product	Notes
			in this month	6-8 weeks			
5-Jun	15-Jun	B Hitchins	2000			Stakeholder	IG to do Q & A
7-Jun		E Co Printers Ltd		1000			MR sending info,to do projection
		P Walker		3000		MTA, FIBs, pp	MR sent replacement form to AK
2-Jun	22-Jun	P Rirchens	2000			IHT	Forms sent to GF 14/5
		R Graphics Ltd		3000		PP & CIC	Mr chased - he sending forms
25-May	19-Jun	O Ogden	1450			CIC, PP transfer	Mtg booked
		P Bentall		3000		Investment	
		S Cray		0		Pension Transfer	
31-May	20-Jun	H Hamilton			1770	LTA, FM ISA	Mtg booked
		C Webber		1000		IHT	
1-May	17-May	E baddmann		500	500	2 x Life Cover	KD to fax LoAs back to us.
2-May	24-May	GamesCo plc	250	250		Group bens	forms sent to MS 07/06
		G Yatter		500		Stakeholder	
11-Jun	5-Jul	M Bedden	100			pp inc, invest	MR sent email re mtg.
		Acme co Ltd		0		Group Bens	
		TOTAL	5800	12250	2270		
					8070	Finish	
			total all list	20320			
			new this month	12450			
			ideal total on list	23000			
			THE GAP	2680			

Diagram 9.1 – The WIP List

and ascertain what business will be definite by calling all the clients and filling the slots in our Success Planner diary. In the first week almost everything should be in the **'Maybe'** column, with the exception of closing meetings already booked, often 'rollovers' from the previous month. It is important to be ruthless at this stage as the temptation is to add a lot of potential business (and we all have loads of 'potential' business) and kid ourselves that we have a great month ahead. To truly understand our business and be honest with ourselves then we must be harsh at this stage. A large number in the **'Potential'** looks great and appeases managers but it is only our own bank balance that suffers if the 'potential' is not translated into actual.

If we do this procedure correctly at the end of the four-week month the completed column should have the same figure that the definite column had at the end of the first week.

If we have also followed the Success Planner and know our averages and we have calculated our activity ratios we should know how much work we need in the maybe column at the start of the month to translate to the completed work we need to pay our bills and make a profit.

For example, if we have a closing ratio of 75%, that is three-quarters of all closing meetings ending in a sale and we need £8,500 per month to hit our target, we should really have £11,333 on our 'maybe' list. If we know our average case size is £500 there should really be at least twenty-three possible pieces of business on our list. This is where the dreaded disease 'big-case-itis' can often strike us down!

We may have one large case of £6,000 on our list so we have less small ones making up our total of £11,333. The law of averages then strikes, as it always will and the big case falls away. Suddenly, we are left with not much month left and a big hole in our finances.

The totals on the WIP list also help us. The first is the overall total, which we have already discussed. I find it useful to track the new potential added in the current 4-week period. This avoids constant 'rollover' where we always have cases hanging around that seem to have been there forever. Again, a harsh reality on occasion but necessary to keep us from slipping into the comfort zone we all love so dearly!

The last figures show us if there is a gap in what we need, translated: cash flow problems ahead! If the gap is there we need to add more to the 'maybe' list and convert it to definite and completed.

Although scary the WIP list can be an advisers best friend, especially if used daily, honestly and in conjunction with the opportunity grid in Chapter 3. The figures do not lie to us and as long as we don't lie to ourselves either, the WIP list will be an invaluable addition to our daily statistics and long-term business profitability.

Agendas

Always take an agenda into a meeting, there is a sample in Diagram 9.2. On a very simple level it oozes professionalism. It also serves to keep us on track. Even the best advisers can find themselves distracted or going off at a tangent from the aim of the meeting sometimes. Agendas can also be used as effective tools for other purposes, for example have 'Referrals' as an item somewhere near the end. That way we have no excuse for arriving at 'wimp junction' and not asking! It lets the client know from the outset that referrals are simply part of the normal business process, as natural as 'completing the fact find' and 'any other business'.

By taking excellent notes in the first meeting and then using the clients concerns on the agenda for the second meeting not only will it ensure that you address the clients concerns (rather than a vague preconceived notion of what we think they might want or our own industry jargon) but it also makes the whole process more understandable for the client as we are using 'their words'. If they talk about wanting to retire in comfort, use that as an agenda heading. For example, Agenda item 5, 'your retirement solution' rather than Agenda item 5, 'personal pension including SERPS'

Always have the last item as 'any other business' or 'final client comments'. Not only is this courteous to give the last word to our client but it also avoids something like referrals being the last item and therefore easier to treat as just another item to be dealt with rather than something to fear.

Once you have started to use agendas you will find you build up a library, so although a little effort is needed at the start, soon they become second nature.

AGENDA

Meeting with F bloggs of Acme Ltd and Ian Green Independent Asset Management

Wednesday 20th February

- Update current position
  - Recap and review previous recommendations
  - Confirm online fund switching
- Reactive fund reports at one-to-one meetings
- Feedback from ACME Ltd
- Discuss and confirm service standards
  - Group presentations
  - One-to-one meetings
  - Joiners - in month after letting us know
  - All communication by email
- Confirm service schedule
  - Suggest 2 days per month
  - Employee education
- Confirm fee agreement
  - See separate engagement email
  - Any other costs outside service schedule
- Plan of action
  - Informing staff (new and existing)
  - What next
- Risk benefits review
  - benefits and timing
- Referrals
- Any other business

Diagram 9.2 – Sample Agenda

Trackers

In the past I would always leave a meeting with a completed fact find and pages of scribbled notes, sticky yellow pads and scrawls on the back of business cards. The result of this semi-organised chaos would be that I often forgot what I had promised to do for the client (thus breaking one of the four referral habits straight away, see Page 47) or that I would misplace a piece of paper with the all important facts and figures. To avoid this I now leave every meeting with a completed tracker (see Diagram 9.3) (see Appendix A-6).

GREEN

INDEPENDENT ASSET MANAGEMENT

Client ____________ Date ____________ Grade ____________

Duration ____________ Fees/Comm ____________ Sales Support ____________

Annual Review Date ____________ Year End Date ____________ Referrals ____________

Immediate Business **Action By** **Details**

1: ______ ____________________ ______

2: ______ ____________________ ______

3: ______ ____________________ ______

Quotes

1: ______ ____________________

2: ______ ____________________

3: ______ ____________________

Future Business

1: ______ ____________________

2: ______ ____________________

3: ______ ____________________

Promises

1: ______ ____________________

2: ______ ____________________

3: ______ ____________________

4. ______ ____________________

5. ______ ____________________

Immediate Actions

1: ______ ____________________

2: ______ ____________________

3: ______ ____________________

Notes:

Next Meeting Date: ________

Diagram 9.3 – Meeting Tracker

This tracker has adviser, client, location and time details at the top. The main body consists of five sections each with room for comprehensive notes and 'who tasks should be delegated to'. Any immediate business is logged, making sure nothing ever 'falls through the gaps'. Any quotations or illustrations needed are listed with the parameters (e.g. Whole of Life or Term, Fund Choice, Retirement Age, etc). Business to be discussed in future is logged and subsequently inserted into the appropriate page of the WIP list.

The most important section is headed **'Promises'**. This is where you note all those things you said you would do. On numerous occasions I have had clients congratulate me on this section. It is obviously very reassuring to see your professional adviser write down something under the heading of **'Promise'**. After all, who wouldn't feel safe entrusting their money to someone who puts all their promises in writing? (Assuming of course we follow them through!) The last two sections are for immediate actions, such as 'send letter of authority for pension' and a spare section for notes. Finally we log the date of the next meeting. This is another simple but effective way of ensuring your diary is never empty as the next meeting is simply entered straight into the Success Planner pages.

By combining the meeting tracker with the agenda for the second meeting, you have a failsafe mechanism to provide complete client satisfaction. Immediate business is taken care of, promises are delivered and future business is diarised and followed up. Additionally, by keeping the agenda and tracker on file it provides a comprehensive compliant audit trail.

CHAPTER 10

BUSINESS CREATION USING COMPLIANCE

There is an old joke that refers to compliance as 'the business prevention department'. It needn't be that way.

Compliance – or at least the sheer weight of it has long been a bugbear of advisers. I decided early on to treat what others saw as a negative as a positive. I sat down and looked at how compliance could be used to generate more business. The end result is that I actually pay extra for my compliance manager to do more than the required regulatory minimum.

My compliance manager does all the normal things you might expect but the following are the methods that I devised to turn my business prevention department into a business creation department.

When complying a case, shortfalls in any areas are logged. As an example, this may be anything from a complete lack of PHI through to not fully funding a pension, from not having a will to a life policy not in trust. These items are then included on the reason why / suitability letter that goes to the client after every transaction. Not only is this watertight from a compliance point of view but also generates more business. Often a client will 'phone upon receipt of the letter asking for quotes or premiums for the identified products. Indeed, in many cases we provide estimates in a follow-up letter. For our example, this letter will typically contain quotes and a key feature document for the PHI, a calculation showing maximum pension calculations and an increment form, a Will questionnaire and a trust document. In the eyes of the client we are providing a superior client service. Even if they choose not to proceed with any of our recommendations they have had the option and we have done our job to the best of our ability.

The compliance manager will also note any policies mentioned in the fact find that we do not have agency for and will send a letter of authority with a covering note explaining that we are only able to provide a complete and comprehensive service if we can obtain complete and comprehensive policy details. By signing and returning the form we can do that, saving the client time that they would have spent collating their policy information. We can also provide a summary statement of all their plans each year.

Another activity that many other advisers consider a chore, I consider a fantastic learning experience. This is the observed meeting. No matter how great I think I am (!) the truth is that there is always room for improvement. By having observed meetings, always with the client's permission, I receive invaluable, impartial feedback on my performance. There may be character traits or habits, that I do not realise I have, that can be noted and erased. There may be improvements that I can make in my posture, body language and pronunciation and there may even be room for improvement in my sales, technical and product knowledge!

We even provide clients with the option of completing an anonymous feed-back form, to be returned direct to the compliance manager, so that if there are any areas they feel would improve our client service, the compliance manager can feed-back to me in a regular review meeting. This ongoing and constant striving for improved client service is a major factor in our business and although I cannot prove that it has increased sales or client retention, I am certain that it has.

CHAPTER 11

GOALS

As I sat down to write this section I wondered how I could possibly do justice in one chapter to a subject that has probably had more books and tapes dedicated to it than any other. So, I decided not to compete and instead in the Appendix you will find suggested further reading. Instead I decided to apply The Success Plan principles of pulling together all the best and most efficient pieces of information and distil them into an easy to use practical tool.

Assuming no prior knowledge of goals or as a basic refresher, all goals must be S.M.A.R.T. That is Specific, Measurable, Affordable, Realistic and Timed. Without these parameters goals are simply dreams or fantasies.

The format that I have for goals naturally leads you to set goals with these parameters. All you have to do is go out and purchase your own goal book. It doesn't have to be fancy, just large enough to contain your descriptions and progress towards your goals.

Open out the book so that a double page spread faces you (see Diagram 11.1 overleaf). Split one page horizontally across the middle and split the second page into three columns. These columns should be headed:

- Next Step
- £ Required
- Date Completed

In the top section of the horizontally split page you will stick a picture of the goal you wish to achieve, for example your dream house or new car. If the goal is financial I suggest a cheque made out to you with the amount written in. If the goal is less materialistic and unsuited to pictures a degree of lateral thought may be involved. If you want to lose weight, maybe a previous picture of you when you were that weight or a faceless picture of a model with the body shape you want. If the goal is more spiritual more thought still is needed. It may be to see distant friends more often or to meditate each day.

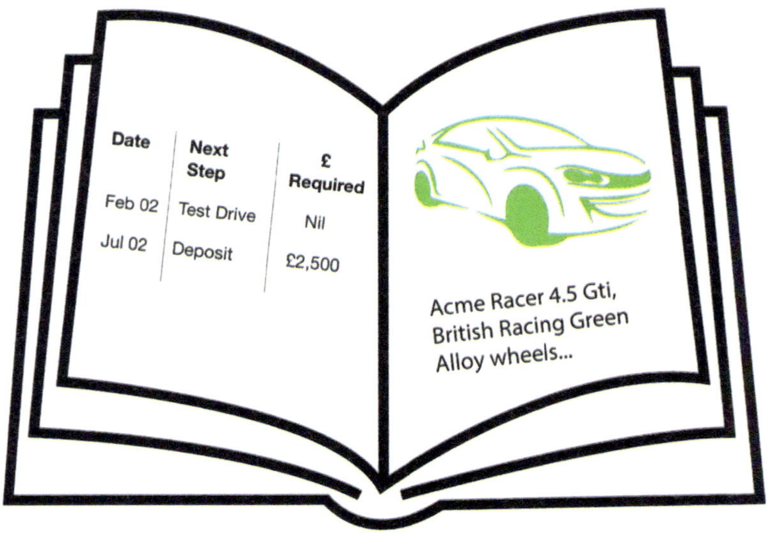

Diagram 11.1 – The Goal Book

Use an image that means something to you, maybe photos of the friends or a section of a map. For meditation a picture of a quiet room or an advertisement from the paper advertising the class you want to visit. There are no firm rules as long as the picture works for you.

In the space below the picture write your description. This is where you really specify what you want. For this reason a short sentence or vague statement really won't do. Instead of 'a new car', describe the car in full, using as many senses as possible. Try to make it come alive. Describe the make, model and colour, the features it has, the type of engine, the extras you'll buy and so on. You may also wish to note the implications of achieving, or not achieving the goal as a further assistance to your mind. This will depend on the goal and if you are more motivated by pleasure (having something) or fear (not having something). If the goal is to lose weight you might write. "I weigh x kg, I have a waist measurement of x cm and I go to the gym three times a week. I only eat nutritious sensible food three times a day. I fit into my summer wardrobe clothes (pleasure) and I do not get out of breath when running for the bus (fear)"

Note how the goal is written in a positive manner, as if it has already happened – "I weigh x kg", not "I want to weigh x kg" or "I will lose x kg". Stating it in this fashion lets the brain accept it is possible and work towards it rather than letting the brain think you'll do it one day.

The first page ensures the goal is S – specific, as we have a picture and a detailed description.

The page with the columns takes care of M – measurable. You start by writing a description of the next step to be taken to advance you towards the goal. If your goal is a new car, the first step might be to obtain a brochure. This way, whenever you feel like achieving or moving towards a goal you have an immediately accessible action plan for each of your goals. This is especially useful if you are feeling down, as there will undoubtedly be a quick action that you can take to advance you towards one or more goals and get you feeling back on track again.

It is a good idea, if possible, to list as many stages of your goal as possible. So, with the car example it may be buy a car magazine, order brochure, arrange test drive and so on. Of course, with some goals you won't be able to plan the next step until the previous one is completed.

The second column is to note the cost of any stages. The next stage in the car example could be to place a deposit to order the car. Naturally this will need money so by listing it here you have a forward planning tool that can be used in conjunction with the Success Planner and your Business Plan to make sure the goal is A-affordable.

The last column is for the date when you complete the step. This gives you an ongoing progress chart for your goals. Another use for the column is to set deadlines for achieving the task. Alternatively, you can place the deadline for reaching the goal at the bottom of the page, once again written in a positive fashion. By giving a deadline and logging the date each step is completed then you ensure the goal will be T-time orientated.

That just leaves R – realistic. But then who am I to say what is a realistic goal for anyone else. If you believe strongly enough in the goal and you follow the other steps I have no doubt you will achieve your desired result. Just be wary of setting yourself a goal that is too unrealistic. If you are aged 94 and have never run a race in your life becoming the Olympic 100m sprint champion is unlikely – not impossible – but definitely a sizeable task!

One last tip. Only share your goals with those you feel will share your ambition. Too many times dreams are stopped in their tracks, often before they have even really begun, trodden into the ground by negative people. These negative people are sadly the majority in the world, but the truth is that if you follow the goal setting principles in this chapter and take action (you must take action as a goal without action will remain but a dream) then you will achieve your aims. Don't let the ill-chosen words and actions of others deter you. Choose only to share your goals with those who will support you and your dreams will come true.

Take the principle of breaking down goals and achieving them step-by-step into all areas of your life. In Chapter 5 we looked at breaking down your annual target into average case sized chunks. Why not set mini goals on the way to larger aims. If you want to lose weight reward yourself with new clothes at various stages rather than punish yourself by waiting until the very last moment. By doing this we help ourselves to have a sense of always moving forward and not stagnating. And if, on rare occasions, you do seem to have come to a standstill on a goal, you may decide it is not something you want anymore. However, it is much more likely that you will return to your goal book and take action on the next step written in order to get it moving again.

SECTION 4

CHAPTER 12

MY STORY – PLATFORM TO PLATFORM AND ZERO TO 1,500

I had been a tied adviser for four months. I was doing OK, progressing up the hierarchy of the life company and starting to 'be noticed' by the management but in truth amounting to nothing special. I remember sitting on a railway platform one afternoon, having travelled miles to visit a new prospect only to arrive and find no one in. I hauled myself back to the office resigned to a session on the telephone. I picked up a fax that had been put in my in-tray by mistake. It was a letter inviting the adviser to go to a local LIA regional meeting (see Appendix A). As I handed it to the intended recipient I asked if I could go along with him. I was feeling dejected after my wasted client trip, thinking I'd rather do anything than start to make cold calls and in fact the content looked rather interesting. My colleague barked that he wouldn't be wasting his time going to the meeting, especially with a lowly trainee (he had a prior engagement to attend to with a Mr Jack Daniels at the bar downstairs I later found out) and I was welcome to the invite.

I was amazed at what I saw and heard. Two speakers, both advisers, both clearly hugely successful in the business sharing all their ideas and explaining how to do what they did! But how could this be? Everyone in my office jealously guarded their operational modes and client file cards were kept under lock and key.

I still have the notes I made to this day. I picked up a leaflet on the way out and posted my application form for membership of the association the next day. Along with my first monthly magazine came a call to attend the annual conference with a dazzling list of speakers. I thought that if the local meeting was that good then what would the national convention hold for me?

Penniless as I was I booked myself into a top hotel and purchased my conference ticket. I arrived early, pinned on my name badge and watched the registration hall fill up. I seemed to be the only one there on his own. Everyone else was chatting with old friends and mingling in groups. Eventually I decided that I would have to make the first move and sat down on the last remaining chair next to a gentleman filling out his attendee's pack. His body was turned away from mine, so I cleared my throat to attract his attention and to break the ice I asked whether if like me, this was his first time here.

As he turned to face me the ribbons and regalia attached to his badge (and those that have attended any conference will know what I mean) nearly took my eye out!

I had unknowingly accosted a past president of the association and one of the most highly respected members of the industry. After he stopped chortling at my innocence and wiped away the tears of laughter he took the time from a busy schedule to acquaint me with the format and with what to expect from the meeting. He advised me that to continue my practice of randomly accosting strangers and to ask them for their best sales idea. He assured me that each and every person I asked would be delighted to help – and he was right. To start my collection of sales ideas he showed me a presentation that I still use to this day. He also promised that if I met him in the evening he'd introduce me to a very close acquaintance of his who would also help me.

The day's events blew my mind. I heard technical presentations, learnt of body language and NLP, goal setting and main platform stories of tremendous courage and victories against the odds. Still reeling I went to the pre-arranged meeting place. I was introduced to a successful London based IFA. What was supposed to be a quick social introduction turned, as is so often the case, into a long evening and the beginning of a friendship and new chapter in my career.

Before I tell that story, the lessons to be learnt from the above are what make this profession so amazing and special.

Take time out for your own education. It is not an expense, but an investment in the best performing asset there is – you.

Unless you have learned all there is to know continue to go to your local regional association meetings. If you used to go, why did you stop? Try it again. Pick the brains of those that are there and the speakers too. It is all organised by people wanting to put something back into the profession from which they earn their living. They give their time and services freely to help others in the same way they were themselves helped. Even dare to be involved yourself and offer to help.

I have never heard of any other industry anywhere in the world where the absolute top performers will reach down and put out a hand to help others up alongside them. It is these attributes that keep the profession so strong in the face of constant regulatory change and repeated adversity from sections of the press.

The time spent that evening culminated with a decision to meet again outside the conference when we were both back in London. A sociable outing eventually turned into an invitation to join the company. My new mentor had done something else I'll never forget. He put his reputation on the line for me. Against the wishes of his three business partners he insisted that I should be given a chance. Nine months after starting in the business I was an IFA.

On my first day he promised me all the help I would need to succeed. But he also quoted me an old adage "Give a man a fish and you feed him for a day. Teach a man to fish and you feed him for life". He would teach me everything but there were to be no fish thrown in.

I learnt about glass ceilings too. At the life company I was considered successful in my peer group. Suddenly I was thrown into a group where the minimum acceptable standard was twice the level I was operating at. But that was the key to the first big jump in my production. It was the minimum acceptable. No fuss, just do it. So I did. I didn't intend to let myself or my new mentor down. My first month's production was five times what I had ever done before. In one month I completed 50% of what I had taken the previous nine months to achieve. Why? Because that is what we did.

From that point on I continued my habits that had stood me in good stead so far. I worked hard, very hard, but I also learned constantly. I was in the enviable position of being surrounded by four of the top, per capita, producers in the country. As long as I respected their time, they helped me without question. In time other advisers were bought in which helped to raise standards and as the bar continued to be raised, so did my minimum acceptable standard. My mentor was gracious enough to mention me and my achievements in a main platform presentation he gave, this remains one of my proudest work memories to date.

By realising that everyone around me had good and bad points and by aiming to replicate the good bits and ignore the bad bits I was able to get a very clear picture of what makes a successful financial adviser. Each successful in their own way and I was able to pick and choose what I wanted from that. Just by being around them, hearing what they said on the phone, how they booked appointments, watching how they looked after their clients gave me an education money cannot buy. It is something that is not learnt in FPC or AFPC and it doesn't come with a financial services degree. Those qualifications are important, but they are not what I learnt. On top of the business education I also received a great grounding in life. I strongly recommend that anyone new in the profession and reading this book, finds themselves a mentor to help them. I was lucky – I had four. Others from this time remain close friends and one is now Godfather to my son. In turn I am now mentoring someone through the MDRT/GAMA initiative and it is my hope that he will succeed by his own definitions and in turn help another.

But time marches on and my life was changing. I was recently married, my son was about to be born and I felt I wanted a new challenge. My time at the IFA in London was incredible. I was privileged to learn from some of the best IFAs in the country.

I had started to speak at LIA regional meetings and write articles in the financial press. I was also regularly appearing on TV and radio as a financial commentator. This was another tip I had picked up from a fellow speaker at an LIA regional meeting. Another fine example of win-win. The media outlet gets an expert as an authoritative source and we, as advisers, gain exposure and credibility.

At my new company we were encouraged to attend MDRT. In fact given sufficient production and qualification for membership the company generously subsidised the ticket and air fare. I had seen people with badges at the LIA conference with MDRT on and one of the strangers I had accosted had gone on to introduce me to no less than the president of MDRT who was a speaker at the conference.

Having met with the president and due to a desire to see for myself exactly what MDRT was all about, I attended the annual meeting, that year being held in New Orleans as soon as I qualified. Three years on I was as amazed at what I saw there as I had been at my first UK conference. Speakers made me laugh out loud and others made me cry. I mingled among 6,000 people from over 50 nations. The same rule applied. I could ask anyone anything and they would share their ideas. A ribbon on their badges marked out the Top of the Table members (see Appendix A) as the top 0.1% of the financial services industry. The *crème de la crème*, all sharing their tips with me. In addition my badge was coloured differently so as to identify me as a first time attendee. The result of this was that total strangers would stop me and congratulate me on my achievement. Picture the sight of a slightly embarrassed lone Englishman having his hand shaken and being back slapped by a pair of enthusiastic Texans and you are some way to imagining the scene!

I came back to England full of ideas and feeling ten feet tall, a changed and improved person for the experience. I resolved to return and ultimately attain Top of the Table Status.

One day, a few months after my wife had given birth to our son, I received a call asking if I would be interested in submitting a manuscript for approval by MDRT and if successful, to speak at an afternoon session in Toronto, Canada. It seemed that by simply giving rather than taking

I had been 'noticed'. That person, like so many before, was putting their reputation on the line by giving me the chance to perform at the premier financial services conference in the world. Again, I am truly grateful and indebted to them. As ever I decided I would not let myself or them down.

Imagine being asked to speak at the MDRT annual meeting? I couldn't believe it! I worked night and day on my presentation and eventually learned I had been successful. I practised and practised until the big day arrived. The past president, who I had first met four years previously, generously agreed to moderate my session. The theatre was filled with 1,500 people, some with headsets on to listen as the words were translated into other languages. Although it passed in a blur I remember walking off as the applause was subsiding thinking that was the most incredible event in my professional career so far ...

EPILOGUE

It was due to the kind words and encouragement of so many that I wrote this book. It will be a proud moment for me as it goes on sale for the first time at an MDRT annual meeting where I have been asked to return as a speaker for the second year running.

So, is this the end of the story?

No, but it is the end of this book. But for me, it is just the beginning of another chapter. As I experience more I find that I have an ever-growing goalbook of dreams to realise and goals to achieve.

I've written about how I went from having no one to speak to, to speaking to 1,500 people at once. I hope to progress and look forward to speaking to thousands more all over the world, both in person and through these pages, in the hope that I can pass on some of the knowledge that has rubbed off on me over the years.

If you feel that you have learned anything from these pages then please pass the information on to someone else and help them too. Thank you for reading this book.

I wish you every Success.

THANKS

As with all pages of this nature to be comprehensive is nigh on impossible and there will always be someone missed out.

I would like to thank those that took the time to read the manuscript and provide such ringing endorsements and to all involved in the editing and publishing without whose gigantic efforts these words would not have seen the light of day.

The individuals described in this book will know who they are, what they have done for me and how I feel about them. I thank them all. I also thank the people involved in my career to date that space prevents me from mentioning individually. They too know who they are and what their help has meant to me.

I'd like to thank all those who helped during my time at the tied agency, all those who influenced me while at the London IFA and those that work with me now. Running the business would not be possible without them.

Thanks to my friends and colleagues in professional associations across the UK and the world, who share their ideas so freely and readily and who encourage and teach me in so many areas.

My clients deserve thanks and I consider it a huge compliment that I count clients as friends and friends as clients.

My parents for helping me to become the person I am and being there at any time.

And my son Max – because he is.

APPENDIX A

ASSOCIATIONS AND IDEAS

MDRT – Million Dollar Round Table. Acknowledged by many as the premier organisation in the world for financial advisers and life insurance agents. Membership is possible by achieving a qualification level set and increased each year. The 'Top of the Table' is six times this level. Advisers belonging to MDRT must abide by a strict code of ethics pledging to place the interests of their clients first.

LIA – Life Insurance Association. An organisation representing the majority of advisers in the UK. At the forefront of representing the profession with regulators and government and keen promoter of continuing education through a program of regional meetings.

A-1 I first heard of the opportunity grid from an adviser at an LIA regional meeting in Essex. However I also later came across it, albeit with a different title, on 'The Achievers Edge' audio cassette by Peter Thompson, a leading UK sales trainer. I apologise if this idea originated outside financial services and was previously published without my knowledge.

A-2 The coloured diary system is an expanded version of The Time Log, taken from my notes at an LIA London regional meeting presented by Ken Clark, co-founder and past president of the LIA.

A-3 I heard the ideas for sending out a mini fact-find and presenting a successful seminar from Leo Millward of Legal & Financial Planning based in Lichfield, England

A-4 This idea was presented by Alessandro Forte in a presentation at an LIA UK annual conference and later produced in their membership magazine, Prospect

A-5 Taking an inventory of your activities with a view to delegating them and the Referability Habits™ were ideas I read about in 'How The Best Get Better™' by Dan Sullivan and published by The Strategic Coach®. I have since started The Strategic Coach Program in Toronto and this is a step I would encourage any adviser to consider. Full information on the Program can be obtained from The Strategic Coach, 33 Fraser Avenue, Suite 201, Toronto, Ontario, M6K 3J9, Canada. Tel 416.531.7399 email info@strategiccoach.com

A-6 The original calculation showing at least 50% of your production in a year (it is often nearer 80%) comes from Malcolm Kilminster in his book and seminar programme 'New Vision'. This is also the source for the original layout of the 'Sixty referrals'. I urge any reader to purchase this book or contact Kilminster Coaching for more information. Although taking minutes at a meeting has long been a standard practice of many businesses it was Malcolm Kilminster who formulated the headings for the meeting tracker in Chapter 9.

A-7 This process was developed by Clive Holmes, founder of the LIA

A-8 Attributed to William H Alley of Kentucky, USA in the MDRT publication 'Power Phrases for Success'

A-9 Alfred O Granum, respected MDRT member and representative of NorthWestern Mutual Life in the USA. Responsible for original research generating these statistics

The Daily Points System – My research led me down many paths. It seems this system has been used in many forms for many years and appears in many presentations. In my own files I found it scribbled on a scrap of paper from my first life insurance convention in 1996. It was given to me by one of those I approached asking for their best sales or efficiency idea.

APPENDIX B

FURTHER READING

Financial Services
It Can Only Get Better. Tony Gordon
New Vision. Malcolm Kilminster
The 21st Century Agent. Dan Sullivan
The Feldman Method. Andrew H Thomson

Prospecting
The Power to Get In. Michael Boylan
The Promise of the Future. Duncan MacPherson

Finances (your own!)
The Richest Man in Babylon. George Clason
The 4 Laws of Debt Free Prosperity. Blaine Harris & Charles Coonradt
Think and Grow Rich. Napoleon Hill

Delegation
The Power of Two. Gina Pellegrini-Crist

Personal Development
Being Happy. Andrew Matthews
Unlimited Power. Tony Robbins
Awaken the Giant Within. Tony Robbins

One for the Dads ...
The Sixty Minute Father. Rob Parsons

Goal Setting
The Sky is Not the Limit. Malcolm Kilminster
Goals. Zig Ziglar

Customer/Client Service
Moments of Magic. Shep Hyken

ABOUT THE AUTHOR

He began his life insurance career in 1996. After five months as a tied adviser he became an Independent Financial Adviser (IFA). He now runs a successful practice in London, England working primarily with company executives, business owners, the retired and the retiring.